The last part of the book faces squarely up to the damage done by ethnicity both to the American college and American society. Here the author is not afraid to instance a plural range of dangers, from the activities of HEW (Department of Health, Education and Welfare) to Black anti-Semitism at the student level. There is a fair and full evaluation of open admissions at a large municipal college.

Finally, *The End of Education* investigates the whole liberal drive to self-damage, the instability and insecurity (not to mention excitability) of an entire intellectual class. In thus examining the psychopathology of academic dissidence, this book deserves a place beside Julien Benda's noted *La Trahison des clercs* of 1927.

Since it is now calculated that half of our children go to college, with the U.S. Office of Education projecting a rate of over 60% by 1980, this book comes as a timely and important warning on behalf of parents, as well as educators. Last but by no means least, the humble taxpayer who is footing the bill for this passion for and expansion of higher education will find useful ammunition here with which to ward off the constant onslaught on his pocket in the name of public funding of what is sometimes no less than miseducation.

L.C. 75-5172
ISBN 0-498-01750-8

Printed in the U.S.A.

The End of Education

The End of Education

Geoffrey Wagner

South Brunswick and New York: A.S. Barnes and Company
London: Thomas Yoseloff Ltd

A. S. Barnes and Co., Inc.
Cranbury, New Jersey 08512

Thomas Yoseloff Ltd
Magdalen House
136-148 Tooley Street
London SE1 2TT, England

Library of Congress Cataloging in Publication Data
Wagner, Geoffrey Atheling.
The end of education.
1. Public universities and colleges. I. Title.
LB2328.6.W33   378'.0092'4   75-5172
ISBN 0-498-01750-8

PRINTED IN THE UNITED STATES OF AMERICA

A great licentiousness treads on the heels
of reformation.
—Ralph Waldo Emerson (1841)

Look at them standing there in authority,
The pale-faces,
As if it could have any effect any more.

Pale-face authority,
Caryatids,
Pillars of white bronze standing rigid, lest the skies fall.

What a job they've got to keep it up.
Their poor, idealist foreheads naked capitals
To the entablature of clouded heaven . . .

See if I don't bring you down, and all your high opinion,
And all your ponderous, roofed-in erection of right and wrong,
Your particular heavens,
With a smash.

—D.H. Lawrence, "The Revolutionary"

Contents

Introduction: A View from Magdalen Tower   9

From Excellence to Impotence

    1   An Illiberal Education   31
    2   Student versus Teacher   42

A Trial of Force

    3   The Riots   53
    4   The Criminal as Hero   83
    5   The Collapse of the Curriculum   100

Liberation: Opening the Gates

    6   Open Admissions   125
    7   Remediation   142
    8   Grading   155
    9   The Academic Supermarket   170

Racecourses of Academe

    10   The Race for Racism   181
    11   I, Too, Am a Minority   189
    12   Affirmative Apartheid   212

Epilogue: Down with Us!   231

Introduction:
A View from Magdalen Tower

It was a cold October morning. A man of about fifty-six, wearing a dark suit and a green baize apron, toiled up the last of some worn wooden stairs with a bucket of coal and a jug of hot water. He knocked on the door, received a sleepy response from within, and went in through to the bedroom where he placed hot water in the ewer on a marble washstand. A tousled head turned on the pillow.

"Morning, Hall."

"Morning, sir. Cold out."

"What's it like?"

"Russians playing up again, sir."

"Two eggs for breakfast, please, Hall."

"Scrammies as usual, sir?"

"As usual, please."

"You dining in tonight, sir?"

"I think so."

The man with the baize apron wheezed off into the main room, where he began to clear the fireplace of the night's embers, relay the fire, and, still on his knees, fill the scuttle with new coal. As he left the room, a sonorous bell—Old Tom—boomed the hour across the rimed grass of the impeccably kept quadrangle. The undergraduate in the bed stirred and got up. Soon his "scout" or servant would be up again with a tray of steaming breakfast, after which it might be pleasant to repair to the library for a while, the Sheldonian perhaps, or take in one of those rather daring lectures by Lord David Cecil on nineteenth-century novelists.

A couple of years after this scene the figure in the bed could be met in a queue outside a Quartermaster's Nissen hut in a bleak London suburb drawing up some disagreeable-looking khaki uniform, and a year after that the tousled head, partially clad in a beret, might have been seen poking out of a tank on the searing wastes of the Libyan, or Cryenaican, desert. After the Japanese war ended, you could meet him at Wembley Stadium walking away in a "civvie" suit with that same uniform in a cardboard box.

Before the Second World War some 4.3% of the population of the British Isles went to a university. The figure for America at the time was close to 25%. The American dream was early founded on a franchise of education for all; a famous Philadelphia workers' meeting of 1830 declared that "there can be no real liberty without a wide diffusion of real intelligence . . . that until means of equal instruction shall be equally secured to all, liberty is but an unmeaning word, and equality an empty shadow." Established under the Morrill Act of 1862, the land-grant colleges began a form of open admissions, a place in college for any student carrying a high school diploma, the end result of which will be explained below.

Today we are bombarded by educational statistics from government agencies. It is still hard to be precise about what percentage of Americans ranks as collegiates, because the figures you choose force you to define the university itself, and to call a two-year community college an "institution of higher learning" is inadmissible to some, as is, for others, the exclusion of a school of music or dance that gives humanities courses (like New York's Juilliard). Certainly there are close on three thousand true institutions of higher education in America today and a Department of Health, Education and Welfare figure of college attendance gives 43% in 1973.

Multiversity was the neologism for the huge new American academic entity coined for the University of California at Berkeley by Clark Kerr, then President, who was to say that he left his job as he came to it, "fired with enthusiasm." Today the free municipal City University of New York (CUNY) enrolls over a quarter of a million educationally ardent souls (the statistics can be juggled, but when you want fiscal support you cite masses). At the time the scene in the bedroom above was taking place, the student population of Oxford and Cambridge combined, and of both sexes, was well under five thousand. Today in America we boast, officially, that "half of our children go to college," the Census Bureau reporting in 1970 that those with at least a high school diploma have risen from 38% in 1940 to 75%. Of our college population Blacks are now said to comprise 12.3%, which is above their population proportion. The U.S. Office of Education has already projected 60% of Americans going to college by 1980. We are thus living at the educational high point of American history, 35,000 doctorates having been earned in 1972 alone and over half a million college professors drawing salaries from coast to coast. A sobering thought, when you consider that the majority of the last are publicly financed.

The U.S. Office of Education issues its projections of future college enrollments on the assumption that they mean something, namely that the more Americans we can persuade to prolong their occupancy of classroom seats the better America will be. Those who decline the syllogism are reactionaries. Why, in France only 16% attend college, in England still only 10%, in benighted Sweden but 18%.

Yet what are the standards concerned? If the grading and certificatory practices of our colleges are what I shall show them to be below, you have merely watched a demographic rather than educational advance. In the process you have astronomically increased taxpayers' bills, since the recent increments in college attendance have been, with us, in publicly funded institutions which, between 1966 and 1972, showed an enrollment increase of 1,159,000 as against 68,000 in private colleges. Finally, you force our cities to face the shadow of default.

It will further be suggested below that an even more dismaying degradation of standards has taken place in the area of the two-year junior or community college, of which so much has been hoped by and heard of from statistic-happy agencies like HEW. These two-year colleges have quadrupled in a decade. One enthusiast tells us that in a recent span of five years one such college was put up every nine days. What does this prove? Do they educate?

They probably don't, but they show increase, and in this field more is always better. Go on increasing education, goes the theory, and somehow or other you improve it. In a dense section of *The Real America,* Ben J. Wattenberg writes:

> In short, the schools, desks, books, equipment, teachers and administrative salaries of the greatest education boom in history was [sic] paid for with *public* dollars, legislated by federal, state and local politicians and transmitted via a massive and often bewildering array of "programs." Accordingly, be prepared the next time someone at a cocktail party tells you that "the programs didn't work." Tell him he's wrong. And if he wants proof tell him to ask the plumber's son who's studying business administration at a community college.

Which, being translated, means: don't listen to the facts, seek emotions. Although it can be shown that one after another of these "programs" has palpably failed, don't believe it. Go on listening to yourself, like a Lyndon Johnson convinced that Chinese Communist money was behind student activists. If you go on saying they have succeeded, they have succeeded. I submit that the plumber's son studying business administration may not be being educated at all; he is being prepared to fit appropriately into a technocracy.

Such analyses as Wattenberg's, above, exasperate rather than console; for I know that, unlike myself, Wattenberg has not been assigned to teach, by an inimical Chairman, something called Business English at the Baruch School in New York, where the best that a teacher of Homer could hope for, in my day, was a certain stoic fortitude on the faces before him. If I could look back dispassionately on a career in public education in America, I suppose I should go along with the prevailing ethos with a shrug—you get hurt if you oppose it—and put myself out to grass as gracefully as might be. But I cannot look back dispassionately. There is too much at stake. Education is being ended in America by Tocqueville's "tyranny of the majority." Produce numbers, and you are done for. We are systematically training our students in worldliness; at Oxford we were encouraged by models of unworldliness.

Hence Oxford was elite. It was the university before it was torn to shreds. It was, as that founder of the evening school, Cardinal Newman, discerned it to be—feudal. Of course it was physically so. You lived in a walled college, illicit egress from which, after ten P.M., could only be effected over spiked gaffs and bits of broken glass or else through, in my own college for a while, a barred window onto a side street, two of said bars being of removable wood painted to resemble iron. It was, in fact, much easier to climb under than over, via a manhole in the street through to a coal cellar. The feudality of the situation was such that the respectful scout in his baize apron, depicted above, had considerable authority over the sleepy undergraduate who, if he failed to sleep in, was promptly reported. Scouts and porters, like proctors, were incorruptible. As an undergraduate you represented only four years of their eventual forty. No kowtowing to the "now" generation on the part of our college servants. I dread to think what "traumas" I suffered there.

In this forgotten feudal unit one's allegiance was to the college as a social whole. Dining in—in my case, under the fat nose and pursed lips of Holbein's Henry VIII—was one of the few compulsions in a life of great freedom, after school (free as mine was). Chapel had only recently been made voluntary. Yet attendance there was still high, even by agnostics, since chapel and hall were principally regarded as expressions of corporate life; also in the former one heard some very pleasant music. Principally, though, one met together. In Roy Harrod's life of John Maynard Keynes we read, of Oxford, "The main part of an undergraduate's education is imbibed from other undergraduates. One may indeed acquire from lectures or laboratories the rudiments of a subject in which one wishes to specialize. But the processes of higher education are subtler; it is a question of what gives the stimulus to the creative or logical powers and of the mode by which the mind makes a transition from the commonplace to the mature outlook. This higher education has to provide our society with men capable of initiating new thought."

Apart from these few social requirements the Oxford/ Cambridge life made almost no demands, except perhaps the most important. American urban students are repeatedly amazed when told that no one ever had to attend any lecture at all at Oxford, your presence was unchecked, and you were merely recommended by a more or less benign tutor to look in at one or two now and again. They are equally astonished when also informed that the comfortable, book-lined suite of rooms Scout Hall visited above—mine were Gladstone's but who has heard of Gladstone?—lacked running water or any heat except the fireplace. Today's American students demand total sexual freedom and free television in the dormitories and free psychiatric guidance outside them. Until the start of this century there were no baths at all in any Oxford college. Even those of us up as late as 1938 remember having a tin hip-bath before the fire, with a cup of tea on the carpet beside, after some afternoon on the Iffley Road football field.

Nor should the feudality of Oxbridge be exaggerated. If it took in chiefly the upper clases (in particular, during one century), it at least educated them, and saved England many a blunder of public policy. It is true that until recently one was selected by the officers of a college as much in interview as examination, but it is equally true that after the Second World War, and before the Labour Government under Attlee had created fourteen new universities in five years, there was a minority of public school boys (read private schools in America) attending Oxford. Of all the colleges only three—Christ Church, Trinity, and New College (thanks in its case to scholarships for those from Winchester School)—had more public than grammar school boys. I recall being interviewed for a job in London at this time. After an auspicious start my invigilator looked down regretfully at my record—"Ah, I thought you said you'd come from Manchester Grammar School."

This introduction is not meant to be an elaborately nostalgic *eheu fugaces*. Such could too easily be dismissed today. But it behooves any book on education to state its premises. It is a curious feature of reminiscences of Oxford life that their authors look back on something other than this heady freedom and normal eccentricity of daily life. It wasn't simply, in other words, crumpets and conversation beside a dying fire, though those ineffectual fireplaces played, one must admit, an almost symbolic role in our lives. It is alleged that a famous American who had been a Rhodes Scholar was revisiting his former Oxford college when a photographer spotted him on the way to his old rooms. The celebrated American was duly sat in a chair and asked to take up a characteristic pose. He reached automatically for a poker—"I'm sure I spent half my time at Oxford poking my fire," he said. One other ingredient was needed: a book. A member of the college pressed one into his left hand. It was Mill on liberty.

This picture—elitist, feudal—may be said to be at one end of the educational spectrum—a vanished and no doubt anachronistic model today. Oxbridge did not in fact attempt to educate in the sense of learning for a definite end. It gave access to a code, through which you found your own. You got a glimpse of the way in which truths are arrived at. Of all the many books attempting to define or catch the essence of the old Oxford life, J. C. Masterman's *To Teach The Senators Wisdom* is to my mind the best. I remember "J.C." long before he wrote this charming book, and was known merely as the author of an amusing detective mystery by the outside world. Later, he was to become Provost of Worcester College, one of the warmest and most modest of personalities imaginable.

His definition of a university is worth quoting at the start of this study of "the end of education" simply because it reads today as the deliberate antithesis of everything the American urban college has come to stand for: "a place of learning, where learning was honoured for its own sake, where those who came loved it, and where the lovers of truth and knowledge pursued their studies without any thought of their ultimate objectives or of positive results." *That* was the essence of Oxford, a moment when one could stand aside and take count, a period for which one would ever be grateful.

It was apparently also the essence of Cambridge ("the other place"), if we are to judge both from its products and a parallel book to "J.C."'s, namely E. M. W. Tillyard's *The Muse Unchained*. Here again we encounter the core of liberal education: the student must never treat facts "as an end in themselves; he must ever subordinate them to ideas. And those ideas must be his own. . . ." The deliberate turning away from Benthamite utilitarianism in this attitude is equally evident in an anecdote "J.C." tells of a stocking manufacturer who came up to him in search of someone likely to go into his business: "What sort of man do you want?' I said. 'A first in Greats [classics],' he replied. 'I've never been to Oxford or to any other university, but they tell me that the first in Greats is the man with the best brain. I can teach him all the technical knowledge he requires, provided he has a keen and adaptable brain.'" Equally, at Cambridge the English Tripos was established only in 1917 and an English degree was fully possible only nine years later. The Classics would teach you all you wanted to know or, rather, be (they have all but vanished from the American curriculum today). Virtually only a handful of Ph.D.'s in English were awarded at Oxford and Cambridge before World War Two (and, frankly, not much more than a handful thereafter). This is reliably alleged to have been also a reaction against German philological scholarship.

In many ways this ideal has marked important distinctions. It has meant a back turned on sociology by Oxbridge and it proposes that you can have an aristocracy of intellect, to which anyone sufficiently intelligent can be admitted, an elite of the mind that survives by virtue of being an elite, its accomplishments of use for the whole community. The functional vocational schools that so many American universities now are emphasized, on the other hand, mastery of areas of knowledge before the grasp of how that knowledge is arrived at and before any understanding of what it means to oneself and others. We would never have rid ourselves of polio without an elite. But the power of discrimination is becoming subordinated to the acquisition of information—doubtless by now a platitude, if one we should remind ourselves of constantly. Yet even by the most vocational standards—and, after all, part of one's vocation is going to be life, living with one's fellow-beings—can one really call what goes on in a large municipal "multiversity" in America today education?

When was the last time Fred Hechinger and his colleagues on the *New York Times* who write so knowingly of higher education sat in a classroom like the one assigned to me today, overcrowded, overheated, an admitted fire hazard, its chairs trashed, obscenities scrawled on the walls, stuck with gum and littered with butts, junkies drowsing blearily at the back, a few girls morosely chewing gum, buffing their nails, and yawning over the *Daily News*, while in front the professor tries "irrelevantly" to recite that revolutionary called Shelley in competition with two airplanes droning overhead, a drill tearing up the sidewalk outside, and two or three transistors blaring rock in that "open-corridor" education advocated so earnestly by Professor Neil Postman of New York University?

Another distinction was that Oxbridge was *truly* contra-cultural. The multiversity is a homogenizing hopper into which you feed high school products for processing into the professions. No wonder it seethes with dissent every so often, since it is thereby negating its own role. At Oxbridge a certain idleness—no examinations for three years—was essential to the general existence; it criticized the value of busy-ness beyond. This has now changed. But there was no television when I was up, and there were only two or three cinemas nearby. Most of us were too poor to import entertainment and so had to provide it among ourselves. You did not have to be artistic to be aesthetic. The dons (take Wittgenstein or, in my own college, Canon Jenkins, who died with two teeth in his head and forty thousand books in his chambers) make the hippiest young academic in America seem feeble by comparison. Here is an accurate picture of Lord David Cecil by a former pupil, George Scott:

> He was an eccentric who delighted visitors with the sight of him in straw boater, flapping splay-footed across the quadrangle, his shoulders and his lank, skeletal frame rolling and swaying with the restless, jerky movement of a marionette. He would turn up for lectures wearing a raggedy maroon sweater, his beard unshaven and his hair uncombed, his head become even more skull-like with dark shadows and deepening furrows. He would forget altogether the times of tutorials although he had sent his pupils a card only the day before. He would lose manuscripts and mislay books and he would cough and speak through a haze of smoke. But the strangest thing about him was his ability to make uncouth boys from secondary schools feel at home with him and their subject.

He was, in short, an eccentric, yet typical. Enid Starkie was another such, sweeping into her lectures on lunatic French poets in long skirts, flaunting feminism and frank over her own lesbianism, but always first and foremost someone it was hard not to love. Such people would never have understood the term *professor* applied to Bruce Franklin of Stanford, finally fired, after long and expensive litigation, for inciting students to violent and illegal acts, a man who came to his hearing replete with pictures of Stalin and Mao, while his wife stood by his side with a rifle. Nor would they have accorded the term to one Cleveland Donald of Cornell, who advised a class to "get a gun and start shooting," any more than they would have to CCNY's Jay Schulman who, when asked on television what his sociological specialty was, answered, "Changing social systems." Quite frankly, beside Lord David Cecil, Bruce Franklin would look, intellectually, like Mary Poppins. For Oxford has long been notorious for suporting lost causes. Its debating Union voted not to fight for King and country a few years before almost every undergraduate, and undergraduette, up at the time was unquestioningly lending a hand to the defeat of Hitler. With the Labour landslide after the war, the same Union went largely conservative, only then to send many of its officers into extreme socialist ranks, including more than one genuine revolutionary to the House of Lords.

The point about Oxbridge was that teaching was never what we in America now principally require it to be. I would much doubt if either Enid Starkie or Lord David could last long in the kind of rat-race institution where now I teach, although I am equally certain both would be revered by so-called "minority" students. How taken aback the young turks of today asking for the abolition of examinations would be to learn that, before the Statutes of 1802, candidates for a degree at Oxford chose their own texts and examiners alike. Virginia Woolf, daughter of a Cambridge don (who once wrote, "What a blessed place this would be if there were no undergraduates. . .No waste of good brains in cramming bad ones"), was particularly persistent in denigrating the idea that literature could be "taught"—and of course by Oxford one means Cambridge. After all, one "read" the literatures; one did not have to be taught them.

Language study at the universities of England half a century ago was textual—almost deliberately inefficient. The idea that meaning might come from sources other than *lettera scripta* was heretical. At Oxford I studied, or rather "read" (the term is significant), modern languages. For modern languages, such as my own German and French, some preliminaries in ancient languages (Greek or Latin) were required.* The "school" bifurcated out of Greats, or the classics, around the turn of the century. One gathers there was

---

*A U.S. Office of Education survey found that in the first two decades of this century half of all American high school students did some Latin; by 1962 this figure had been almost halved; today it is negligible.

a fairly reluctant condescension about the occurrence and, indeed, when I was up, there were no courses given in any literature post-1830; by virtue of stubborn persistence Enid Starkie was able to get up a set of lectures on such improbable characters as Baudelaire and Flaubert, but there were no examination questions on these outcasts.

Today I find myself teaching in a college where almost nothing *before* 1830 gets considered as literature. As recently as 1965 Professor Alistair Campbell, in the Chair of Anglo-Saxon at Oxford, could still say, "English literature proper stops at 1830—after then, it is only books." And, by implication, improper books at that. The recent genuflections to our relevance ritual reverse this premise—*only* books written after 1830 are literature. Then let us, in a few more years, emend that to only after 1930. And so on. For relevance has an open end. To be truly relevant you should study each moment what is momentarily happening.

Does this say anything to those scrutinizing the offerings in English literature in college catalogues in America today? In a short but trenchant essay called "Why?" Virginia Woolf put the question "Why learn English literature at universities when you can read it for yourself in books?" Talking to a friend who had been given the task of reporting to a publisher her opinion of a study of the Elizabethan sonnet, Mrs. Woolf went on:

> All I could gather was that this lecturing about English literature "If you want to teach them English," she threw in, "teach them to read Greek"—all this passing of examinations in English literature, which led to all this writing about English literature, was bound in the end to be the death and burial of English literature . . . do they write any better for it? Is poetry better, is fiction better, is criticism better now that they have been taught how to read English literature?
>
> "But think of all they must know," I tried to argue.
>
> "Know?" she echoed me. "Know? What d'you mean by 'know?'"

Virginia Woolf took here what most today consider to be the strict meaning of teaching, namely pedagogical instruction leading to improved skill in a given field. Her suspicion of the pragmatic is therefore all the more striking. Can you see Virginia Woolf walking in tomorrow to take a city college class, saying "All right, everyone, do your thing," and giving a liberal beam as the transistors at the back were turned up, while the rest of the class wolf-whistled at her?

If you want to understand Swahili, read Greek. German Departments, which are not socially functional in New York City in the way Spanish Departments are, have been finding themselves up against it of late—they are *per se* fascist, in any case. But what happens when it is decided that, as we shall see below, the latest minority claims are Croat? At Oxbridge the point propagated was that your relationship to language should *not* be purely functional, should properly include that to nonspoken classics or "dead" languages. A long Latin letter written from Oxford to the High Master of St. Paul's by one Benjamin Marshall at the beginning of the eighteenth century reads, in part, as follows:

> I rise before dawn, and at six o'clock attend the public Latin prayers. . . . I return home, and from that time shut myself up in private. There I occupy myself with the study of the Minor Prophets. . . . From nine to ten I give my mind to Philosophy, which that Roman orator deservedly calls a kind of progenetrix and parent of all the arts. . . . When it strikes ten I go to my tutor. . . . I return to my room and gird myself for my studies. I apply myself at once to the Koran . . . at last I place Aristotle's *Rhetoric* before my eyes.

It is clear that another attitude—not least that to sheer hard work—is being taken than obtains in today's academy. Anyone, it is presumed, can learn to speak a "modern" language. Such instruction is the function of Berlitz Schools; the product of the Oxford Modern Language School was able to give subtle textual explications of *Faust*, but found himself at a loss in the Speisewagen of his first train to Berlin. During the war in Europe he became envious of the manner in which GI's could transmit meaning to foreigners, despite grammatical inaccuracies he had been persuaded to regard as worthy of the garotte, over sherry in Peckwater Quadrangle. The American attitude to foreign-language learning was far more useful, and perhaps wholesome. Oxbridge was not trying to be useful. The way it taught languages may have been misguided, but it was evidence of an attitude. The whole point of an Oxbridge Arts degree was that it was not, nor ought to be, in the words of J. C. Masterman, "only a measure of a man's knowledge and power of assimilation."

To dismiss the Oxbridge ethic as irrelevant to modern American needs is not merely to miss the point, it is a dodge. One was brought up to be alarmed by the confidence of empirical science. Today the ex-Communist Columbia Professor Robert Gorham Davis tells us in a banner headline, "The Professors Lie." He means to say, where he understands his own argument, that the Humanities professoriat professes to be in search of an objective truth that does not exist. Sidney Hook corrected him, observing that if we charge someone with a lie, we suppose *we* know the truth; the New Left liberal always does.

But men like Masterman and Lord David Cecil, and ladies like Enid Starkie and Virginia Woolf, never made such pretensions; they expressed their vision of truth by despising what was not art; and business, the making of money, was not art, it was scarcely more than a habit. Hence the Oxbridge don was a living anachronism, a genuine activist. The progressively bearded barbarians who staff the humanities at our municipal colleges, and strut in packs now to Moscow, now to Peking, are the reverse; backed by their praetorian guard of rioting students, they are in league with the philanthropic and agnostic democracy beyond the gates. Indeed, they are breaking down those gates to let technocracy, and its kind of truth, inside.

This civilization has been called, by an anonymous writer in *Midway* magazine, "more tightly feudal and mercantilist than it has ever been." The paradox obtains because, in modern urban America, the destruction of repressive organizations has turned into a tradition—perhaps a pastime. It is a red herring to object that the medieval academy, or Harvard, was originally in service to its society by virtue of being a theological seminary; theology supposed a God, whereas ours is "the people." And to educate the people for a technology, you have to impose limits and protections and hindrances, which at the same time you are obliged to destroy since they appear authoritarian. The contemporary academic liberal thus finds himself constantly treading an ideological quicksand.

Since the French Revolution art has been called on to house and safeguard the last elements of sanity, in the iron face of the advancing Frankensteins of industry. Baudelaire thought it could offer man salvation. Shelley wanted the poet to be a legislator. Nietzsche hoped that art could redeem life. By the end of the nineteenth century, as the *Midway* contributor puts it, the song of the poet-prophet had become "a perpetual *sursum corda*." Enlightened Europe conceded that civilized values were located in art alone. The Jekyll of science kept improving man's natural estate, but its Hyde kept on, like cancer, taking bites out of civilization—at Hiroshima, Nagasaki, Vietnam.

One cannot put history into shorthand like this, but it is surely safe to say that in New York City today liberalism has become unquestioningly institutionalized and has nothing more to say. Except "shut up." Our tradition is to have no tradition, and be proud of it. The bourgeois Buddenbrook family fell one by one, like rotten teeth, to the religion of art over half a century ago; today our abolitions and permissions have removed all boundaries. Simone de Beauvoir describes what it was like to grow up in the inception of this climate: "We had no external limitations, no overriding authority, no imposed pattern of existence. We created our own links with the world, and freedom was the very essence of our existence."

How, then, can anyone call this state of affairs "feudal"? Because with dissent institutionalized, as it is on the liberal campus, you cannot dissent from dissent (unless you also wish to do so from the payroll). Because the patterns and rules and constraints that have to be accepted (our taxes, exams, laws, dues) arise from outside man, not from within him, and are hated. And because, when there are no more enemies to be found, you invent them: you call a college that had an enrollment of 36% Black students in an area with a lesser minority population "racist." You see "slavery" in the imprisonment of men who have killed bank guards and police, as well as their fellow-citizens. You call painstaking attempts at racial emancipation "genocide." In *Working Through*, Leonard Kriegel, a City College of New York professor, is frank enough to admit as much: "We used the word *genocide* to describe everything from Vietnam to questions of whether college administrations had the right to call police on campus."

Finally, when there are no more prisoners left to liberate, you fight yourself. You have to. For still the great liberal society does not seem to be working as you would wish, seething as it is with discontent and violence at its edges. You run out of straw dogs and Aunt Sallies and, in frustration, turn on yourself. We shall examine some of these self-destructive impulses in the pages that follow. For what has been going on in the liberal American academy is, in its way, a little religious war. Daniel P. Moynihan has said: "I would offer, from the world of politics, the thought that the principal issues of the moment are not political. *They are seen as such:* that is the essential clue to their nature. But the crisis of the time is not political, it is in essence religious." Having lived through this war, and somehow survived its liberalism *in extremis,* I hope to try to show something of what happens to an academy that seems intent on destroying itself—all in the name of liberation. The dissolution of this institution has begun. The death-watch beetles are in the rafters, championing freedom and chanting "Power to the People." They are ink-footed insects, this time, draggling themselves about the back alleys of contemporary writing. As Malcolm Muggeridge, another veteran of such wars, has put it:

> I have seen their prototypes—and I can never forget it—in the role of credulous buffoons capable of being taken in by grotesquely obvious deceptions. Swallowing unquestioningly statistics and other purported data whose falsity was immediately evident to the meanest intelligence. Full of idiot delight when Stalin or one of his henchmen yet again denounced the corrupt, cowardly intelligence of the capitalist West—viz., themselves. I detect in their like today the same impulse. They pass on from one to another, like a torch held upside down, the same death wish.

*The End
of Education*

From Excellence to Impotence

1
An Illiberal Education

In a preface to a group of his essays Lionel Trilling stated bluntly that, as a teacher, his allegiance was to the subject, not to the student. This is perfectly proper. I am paid for a certain competence in English language and literature, not for understanding the inner compulsions of Joe Blow yawning his head off in the back row. The comparison is not unfair; I am employed to be a teacher, not a psychotherapist.

However, one has an obligation to be able to impart that knowledge, which does indeed involve an ability in personal communication. This varies in various disciplines. A lab is not conducted like a literary seminar. But the university teacher must be equipped for and capable in the content of the course, not the content of the student. Shakespeare doesn't change. Students do. The natural sciences and the humanities rest on secure bases of given knowledge. They may change. New texts of Shakespeare might be found, or it may be proved that Shakespeare was a woman as well as Francis Bacon. Still, the Shakespeare scholar should be able to function, to impart interest in and knowledge of Shakespeare as well in Utah as in New York City. The students at such institutions might differ widely.

But let me play devil's advocate for a moment; listen to the reverse view, one that lies at the heart of our college educational crisis today—the abandonment of the subject for the student. American education has become urban (England still has some genuinely rural universities, like that of East Anglia). Not only does every major American city have some network of community colleges in or near it, but by now state universities are so huge as to constitute an *urbs* each. What is more, 70% of our private institutions now cluster around cities. Less than one in four college students now live on campus. No municipal college students, of course, do. Congress continues to throw funds into educational programs in cities because city problems are our sickness. In a single, recent year, fifty new urban community colleges opened, most of them thanks to the Higher Education Facilities Act. The student population of the boroughs of New York is something over three hundred thousand. CUNY alone has a student body of a quarter of a million.

Let us listen, then, to an educator who says that the subject is not of first importance, that the student is; and let us subsequently follow just where this path led him, and his university. Buell Gallagher, for some years President of CCNY and sometime Chancellor of the State Colleges of California, an ordained Protestant minister, enjoins the university teacher in his *Campus in Crisis* as follows: "see that kid in the second seat of the fourth row not only as you see him, but as he sees himself. You might just be able to be of service to the eccentric and brilliant adult that lurks behind those frightened eyes. That is your job, Professor."

Needless to linger over this naive sentimentality. It shows how seldom, if ever, our Presidents look into classrooms these days. No eyes there are "frightened" any longer, only (when open) hostile or glazed. Nor does there seem to be too much brilliant eccentricity about, either. One does not finally have to be so unkind as to point out that the kid in the second seat of the fourth row does not have to be there and, in our case, is paying nothing for the privilege.

But the errand of the whole hosanna is extraordinary. The teacher is to be of ancillary assistance, in a sort of psychoanalytical way, to the interests and inner drives of a superior person, the student. It is this social-service attitude that has now called into question the whole concept of a liberal education in America. "The idea of the humanities," writes Frederick Olafson, "survives mainly as the object of a rather ritualistic piety and as though time were being taken off from the regular business of academic life for the purpose of some rather solemn observance which we are assured will do us a lot of good." Education for a Gallagher is so much social repair, not to say reparation. He even excuses foul behavior on campus: "Good manners, which had been the hallmark of the middle-class Black *bourgeoisie*, were regarded by the newly arriving proletarian as signs of weakness and lack of race pride"—as though you were to be proud of being constantly belligerent, politeness being servility.* Or, as Caliban had it, "You taught me language; and my profit on't/Is, I know how to curse." In this operation, then, a study of the humanities turns into so much self-interpretation, essentially marginal to science. I propose that this is illiberal. The recent reform of our curriculum, I shall also hope to show, is broadly anti-humanistic.

---

*By this point one needs to interject some principles of orthography. In the use of capitals for various groups, a writer has to beware of being as silly as he might be in treating every student as a **she**. Years ago, back in the early fifties, the old NAACP started a campaign to induce publishers to use capitals for Negro. More recently, no less a personage than Denis Brogan made a craven apology, in 1967, for writing this word without a capital; he did not proceed to write White. On this basis I have here used capitals for Negro, Black, Puerto Rican, Italian, and White, except in those instances where lower case was used in original quotations and so had to be respected. Moslem/Muslim creates difficulties since there is no proper noun from which the English is derived.

American general education reposes not on two cultures, but on three. There are the natural sciences, based on laws and concepts. There are the humanities, which loosely include literature, history, philosophy, music, art, and so forth, and which study, in a much more subjective way, to be sure, given bodies of work. There are fringe-benefit subjects, like linguistics, which cross-pollinate both areas and cannot perhaps easily be pigeonholed in either. There is then a third "discipline," further over on the spectrum of subjectivity, and very foreign to anyone brought up in England before the last war, namely social science. The very term seems self-negating; society is not scientific. It is said that sociology is a particularly American heresy; Margaret Mead, I believe, once suggested that Americans have substituted anthropology for history. This sounds about right. Lacking a chronological depth, our society views itself in width (how they do it in Oshkosh); when television came to England it was generally viewed as a historical phenomenon, while in America the viewing habits around the country tended to be the principal focus of interest. The issues of *Public Opinion Quarterly* began to fatten on the topic.

American sociology always baffles Europeans, and perhaps Englishmen in particular. It seems to be a subject of study, rather than an object of study. You are more or less occupied with what you do. Of course, you also study what you *did*, but in the social sciences your personal concerns are preeminent; this is not the case in literature where we must respond to what is central to the work itself, not simply understand ourselves. If there are fifty different views of Shakespeare's *The Tempest* in a single class of fifty, you reach a kind of anarchy in which the work in question barely need have been written. The *Iliad* may help me to understand myself but I cannot empathize with its author (or authors), any more than I can with either the author or characters of

The Brothers Karamazov, in the way I may, and am asked to, in the matter of, say, Urban Social Policy.

The "scientific" quotient injected into such social courses then comes to seem particularly spurious. You are said to be understanding man and society, but what you get taught, statistically, is that all murderers ate mashed potatoes and there exists a percentile possibility you will date the girl next door. Surely the social sciences should be telling us what a liberal education is, but today they do not frankly seem to know. The distinguished Harvard Professor Nathan Glazer is engagingly open about this problem of his own vanishing subject matter:

> I am convinced our first problem as social scientists is not that students are seeking job training, or that they lust for the relevant and the sensational (after all, we should do best at providing that), or that the departments are unfriendly, or that the assistant professors are uninterested—it is that we do not *know*, for reasons themselves tied up with the development of the social sciences, what we should teach as a foundation required of any educated person.

This fog, we shall see, was what made it difficult for the liberal arts professor to see his true enemy in the college riots of the sixties. "The last few decades," declared the President's Commission on Campus Unrest for 1970 (the Scranton Commission), "have witnessed a serious erosion of any clear sense of mission in American higher education." UCLA's John Searle, who served on this commission, added, "though we are now under more pressure for educational reform than at any previous time in my lifetime, most of us are without a coherent philosophy of higher education."

With changing interests making for constant visions and revisions, this lack of security in the social sciences becomes catching; only the natural sciences enjoy a certain immunity from the epidemic. You can have a wave of student interest in astrology, say, with the campus bookstore doing a brisk trade in Tarot cards and the like, but no one seriously proposes substituting courses on astrology for those on astronomy. Alas, and here's the rub, the nearest English Department will initiate a new value-free, but credit-rich, course on the occult. Required reading: Madame Blavatsky's *Isis Unveiled*. No one asks for ephemeral interests in Zen or homosexuality to modify science teaching; but Chairpersons of arts departments will consider it advisable to reflect them, at least for a few years, in their offerings. Under "Art History" my own college's Art Department, I see, offers two courses out of thirty-one on Renaissance Art, one in and one outside of Italy; it lists more courses on film, and still more on contemporary topics. Our Music Department has one course on Bach, rarely given, against several on Jazz, Latin Popular Music, and so forth.

This abandonment of a sequential corpus of knowledge in favor of current vogues will be dealt with more fully in the next chapters; at this point one may say that the movement to serve the student first and the subject second does not apear to be giving anyone concerned very great sustenance. If the social sciences are, as Glazer, an eminent practitioner of them, intimates, "hosts of the hip," then why did a recent Harvard survey of students find them uniformly duller and more time-wasting than the majority of those in the natural sciences and humanities?

In "What Remains of Liberal Education?" in *Change* (Summer 1973), William Petersen cites a study of a college class of 1961 asked to name courses they did not take that they would now like to have taken at college: the chief subjects appearing were foreign languages, literature, English, science, philosophy, and art history. As Glazer comments, it might be more responsive to student interest to have instruction on how to travel in France than on French literature, but can you call such liberal education? He adds, a trifle previously, "One can of course replace Shakespeare with the Beatles, but how often really is that done?" With us it is often done, though not with the Beatles, who are old-hat now; we have courses on rock "poetry" and though it cannot be said that these "replace" Shakespeare in the curriculum, they definitely dilute the bard.

A young professor with an unconvincing Jesus beard and unnecessarily ratty sandals just across the hall from me, a delightful and gifted individual, collaborates with the City Hall educational ethic (and, as a recent appointee, does so understandably) by teaching at least one course from texts that have attained no literary significance whatever—Tarzan books, Rider Haggard, and the like. His argument is that ghetto kids feel overawed by renowned literary masterpieces (far from my experience) and open up more when dealing with Vonnegut or Ray Bradbury. To my mind, this attitude puts the liberal education in question. In fact, it destroys literature; but, of course, in doing so it "liberates" the pleasant young professor, relieving him of the embarrassment of having to defend great works of the past. To go on a field trip to search the Harlem River for evidences of pollution may be admirable ecology, but is it education?

In truth, the latter has been put in question resoundingly in recent years. It has repeatedly been challenged as irrelevant. There seems no way in which we can order the operation without appearing arbitrary. Shakespeare wrote before Milton, but this is a feature of the subject rather than of the inner life of the student, and we shall see that chronology has collapsed as a way of study in many literature departments; and to study the student as your ordering frame of reference, instead of the subject, is to end up with no more than a lot of pluralistic interpretations, and the vicious maxim *De gustibus. . . .* You end up with a collective shrug, so far as the arts go, and thus once more fail your student by not sharpening his aesthetic perceptions for use later in life.

In the city colleges we have been told, and gray heads have earnestly listened, that the liberal arts are simply a tool, an expression, of the ruling class (even when oddballs and disaffiliates like Villon and Defoe come under survey). So Shakespeare and Bach are bilge. Kant is a class privilege. When teaching Chaucer I decline even to bother with the primitivity of this position. I cannot prove Chaucer "useful" to the Gallaghers of this world, and refuse to be trapped into trying. Juvenal dealt with urban problems and Thucydides with ecology, but both would turn in their graves if they heard that that was why they were being read. I cannot even claim that reading Chaucer will do you "a lot of good." Told by a sneering student got up with grenades at the back of class that Chaucer was a White, slave-owning, colonialist lackey of the upper bourgeoisie who worked on the side for a monarch, I can't worry. Next question, please.

However, when the position is indirectly espoused by tax-paid administrators and higher educators, the crisis becomes acute. Are we going to teach the liberal arts at all? Irving Howe, a Hunter professor, has put it: "If you do not believe in the study of literature, don't teach it. If you believe the western intellectual tradition is a manifest colonialism, don't claim to speak for that tradition."

So Chaucer leaves the curriculum (we list him but now rarely teach him); the subject goes, not the student. One realizes that of the three elements in what was long charted for Americans as a liberal education, the middle ground of humanities, the repository of sanity, is being urged into a valueless area repeatedly refounded on shifting sands where there is less and less agreement on what should be taught and where no one, as Glazer observes of the social sciences, seems quite sure what distinguishes the elementary from the ad-

vanced. Surely this situation is serious enough to merit more
attention than it seems to have had.

Economics, and to some extent psychology, require
empirical work, and must be excepted from some of these
generalizations. Both require a degree of mathematical
competence, as also a certain leaven of historicity. You can
say that Keynes was a "fascist hyena" and "running dog of the
imperialists," but you can't say that he couldn't add. Do you
see Coleridge handling his bank statements with equal
confidence? And simply to revert to the history of the
discipline does not help. Everyone before you was a "fascist
parasite," so much "imperialist ectoplasm," anyway, and you
will end up being called the same one day.

To call a liberal education irrelevant is a serious charge.
Made from the comfortable armchairs of city boards of
education, it is more than serious, it is crucial. It affects the
quality of our daily lives. It says that the humanities, in
particular, are not responding to fundamental problems of
our time. The social sciences are. It says that a sense of history
and permanence is inconsequential and that the experience of
a situation guarantees understanding. This is fraudulent. But
Gallagher's "kid in the second seat of the fourth row" is now
presumed to be way ahead of his professors in this direction.
Trilling wrote one devastating polemic, which he delivered to
a scathing audience at City College, arguing that we only
really understand a literature, and a society, if we study one
developing by the side of the other, criticizing and reflecting
and correcting reciprocally over a long sequence of events.

His case was that of England. However, in order better to
expose the crudity of the City Hall mentality in higher
education today, take a group repeatedly subject to exploitation and abuse, and slavery—the disadvantaged, if ever that
word meant anything. Take the *really* oppressed—not
through two centuries or even three, but a race persecuted

with consistency and skill for thousands of years. Are we ready to say that, owing to the "irrelevance" of chronological sequence, to the lack of topicality, the Jews have not given us a transmissible high culture, to say nothing of an enduring moral code? Is all Jewish literature, then, irrelevant, an expression of caste and privilege? Is it, too, to be relegated to our growing heap of the broken toys of academe, all patriarchal, and authoritarian, and racist, and sexist?

One brings to the humanities a degree of interest that is quite different from the passing concerns of daily life. That is why literature and art are serious. As Professor Steven M. Cahn puts it in *The Eclipse of Excellence*, "An education that fails to analyze the nature of capitalism but concentrates instead upon devising plans to increase sales in a local store will not provide the intellectual perspective required to understand economic decisions taken by the government." It might be more immediately helpful to Joe Blow to show him how to work the cash register in the local store; what does that prove? That is reverence rather than criticism of the dominant society. The stocking manufacturer who asked J. C. Masterman for a man who had studied Sophocles was far more percipient; he knew that the Great Greek plays were profoundly enriching and productive of intelligent minds.

Vocational schools have always raised problems, as the Victorians acknowledged. But vocational colleges, almost everywhere in our cities, are something else again. I do not think the like of this philistinism has been seen before in the land and, in the next sections, propose to look at the damage it has done to our curriculum. At my own college no less a personage than the Associate Provost for Institutional Resources, Morton F. Kaplon, writes, "Why do we insist that there exist some common standard of prose for communication when we have available the tape recorder to record and transmit the words we say?" Science will solve everything, including our communication. Meanwhile, it's more important to help Johnny to be able to make change for the subway.

To my mind, there is nothing very liberal about these missionaries. They see themselves engaged in forcible education of the noble savage. Their activities are profoundly destructive of that principle of disinterested intelligence so vital to our society, if it is to survive. For the disinterested study of a subject implies a passionate interest in it, one beside which the ephemeral interests of itinerant students simply pale. As Arthur Bestor has put it: "the scholar who goes after objective data, who weighs evidence, who listens to arguments on both sides, and who is ready to revise his conclusions when an error is revealed—he is not avoiding the world's problems but facing them squarely and honestly. In doing so he is the genuine activist."

Is our whole civic-education complex, on the other hand, to be made over into a gigantic workshop, a hive for future scientists? Each term excited freshpeople, introduced to the poetry of John Donne for the first time, come up to me and ask if they can find a course, somewhere, on Donne. But there shall no Donne be given them. Donne is irrelevant. Try Philo 3: Oriental Religions, or PolySci 5: From Castro to Fanon. For these are very carnally minded missionaries, indeed. At the same time as they say they are opening the doors to all, they are closing those of humanistic study. The aspiration of the latter does not lead to large salaries, cannot be "tracked" to be of proven benefit to the technology. Let us look more closely, then, into the self-mutilation of this liberal mind in action.

2
Student versus Teacher

The vogue for student evaluations of their teachers has been especially American, possibly because the movement is seen as persuasively anti-authoritarian. Oxford and Cambridge professors do not, to date, run around begging their pupils to grade them; even Essex, England's most permissive and politicized university, does not hire and fire teachers on the basis of student opinion of them.

New York City does. It has now institutionalized student evaluations of college teachers, its Board of Higher Education requiring such ratings to go forward with a professor's candidature for promotion, tenure, and continued office. Even part-time instructors must submit to the procedure. The germ of this decision was the November 1970 vote of CUNY's Hunter College faculty to allow students to have a say in the hiring and firing of their teachers.

One does not have to dwell on the expenditure of public money, and time, involved in this operation. Every semester we receive through intramural mail fat sheafs of such evaluation forms, each worthy of the most bureaucratic commissar and accompanied by thirty-six pencils or so, all to be given into the hands of some student trusty who will administer the test and check on us in front of us. In the true manner of

Parkinson's Law these evaluations proliferate annually, creating their own administrative divisions and spawning their own staffs.

I confess that I have not relished those moments of my academic career standing in front of some group of dunces while they sucked their pencils and "evaluated" me, and I understand that our less vulnerable science departments relegate the entire anonymous abracadabra to the nearest trash can. In this they are, I am happy to add, fortified by our union, for whom such evaluations represent unfair practices under labor laws. Unlike faculties, unions are disinclined to whet the knife to cut their throats. As the Jewish saying has it, only the dumbest calves select their butchers.

But the movement goes on, and ever seems to gather steam. As the students gain power they abolish the university; one of the first votes of ours, and they were of graduate students, as soon as they gained control of our Graduate English Committee, was to dissolve the regular graduate examination. As at Antioch, where rioting students who had closed down the college later demanded to be given social science credit for their activities, so at CCNY students appointed to our Curriculum and Teaching Committee moved they be granted college credit for their work on this committee; they complained of so much "outside work" (namely, the normal course of studies). Professor Louis Heller observed that what we were saying was that a student could graduate "just by virtue of having told the faculty how to run the college *even though he himself may never have taken a single college course.*" Why not, by the same token, award academic credit for public service to our Buildings and Grounds workmen? "It took only a few minutes," wrote Heller, arguing this absurdity down the line, "to map out 128 credits for simply being alive—enough for a City College degree."

Each term now some elderly lady with a national reputation will not only have to allow both our faculty and students to appraise her, she must submit to the indignity of having such findings read aloud to her and, at the same time, be asked to show, like a license, last semester's student evaluations of herself. Too often these undignified encounters turn into mutual back-slapping contests. For everyone knows what is really afoot. Nicholas Ratcliffe, a young Chairman of one of our science departments, put it candidly: "The student evaluation process is really a popularity poll and does not indicate the effectiveness of teaching. I'm demanding a drive for work and do not tend to give high grades without justification, which means that I'm not popular." But the process continues, and has now been cemented into the system, partly because hard-nosed boards of education see such evaluations as a *divide et impera* ruse by means of which more easily to keep the faculty in line. That they can be held at all, of course, once more evinces the local professoriat's lack of belief in itself. Old heads on young shoulders, indeed!

In a democracy nobody wants to be in a subordinate position. Unfortunately learners, even adult learners, have to be. The principles of science may change, but they are hierarchical; we must learn them, or remain ignorant. Where authority can more easily be overthrown is in those areas wherein private judgment or bias may be asserted. If governance of a university is in the hands only of those of proven competence, they must be exposed as "elitist" and the institution must be modified. Deriving his ethos from a pragmatic interpretation of how a university should relate to its society, and indebted to political before intellectual criteria, the civic educator will see it as his mission to modify downwards those institutions that come into his purlieu. You do not modify upwards in a contemporary democracy.

What does *downwards* mean? In general terms, the American university is composed of three bodies: the administrative officers, the faculty, and the students. At Oxford and Cambridge the first element was minute, blended in with the second and enjoying very little sovereignty indeed. In a public American college the administrators are, as it were, the external element, suposed to be politically responsible to the constituency and as far as is possible with their regiments of clerks, nonideological. When Harry Gideonse, for example, as President of Brooklyn College, seemed to usurp a degree of personal power over his welfare satrapy, there was much growling in the kennels. Jacques Barzun's *The American University* makes a lonely defense of this element of our academy.

Until recently American faculty enjoyed, by and large, a considerable autonomy. Our own largely hired and fired itself and there were outcries when, as in the case of Bertrand Russell, external pressures overcame us. More recently there have been heard similar outcries against the California Regents for interfering with faculty decisions. We were, for the most part, left in charge of pedagogic affairs. Such a faculty cherished an independence of judgment. Under the halo of self-determination for youth this judgment has now been passed downwards to very young people, and has thereby been considerably qualified.

For what is the position of the student in the triad? Frederick A. Olafson answers as follows:

> it is that of a person who seeks to acquire some definable species of intellectual and/or practical competence through an organized course of instruction upon completion of which his achievement of competence is to be publicly certified by the persons who have supervised his studies and by the institution in which the latter were carried on.

This is a pious hope. Our students are publicly certified by the persons they have publicly certified. Evaluating those who evaluate them, they are in a very ambiguous position indeed, certainly not that of students. Compare the equivalent in medicine. Professor Olafson, in fact, goes on: "it seems clear that if a student is still in the process of qualifying himself in some already existing area of knowledge which has recognized practitioners, he is not in a position to judge the qualifications of the latter for a particular teaching post. If he were, he should not be a student." Yet each term more students are invited to sit in on our faculty deliberations and decisions. These invitations are not always taken up.

If you oppose self-determination of this sort at a municipal college, the most civilized retort you get back is that our students are adults. Certainly society has said they are, able to vote out the Mayor, so why not a disliked assistant professor? The *New York Times* has even advocated pressing more authority of the kind into the eager hands of yet lower age groups. Two out of seven American students are now married—the perambulators multiply in our classrooms—and some of mine are on their second divorces. The rest are doubtless sleeping around in various ways, and positions, God bless them.

And these new adults to whom you are offering your throats will, it is said, be wise enough and fair enough to disqualify themselves as judge and jury when the matter is one requiring thoroughly professional evaluation. Very well. This leaves us simply with their value as human beings, men and women who have had other men and women teaching them. But if the latter have failed thanks to human flaws, why are the former any less likely to show similarly human failings when themselves evaluating?

It used to be a procedure of psychoanalysts to have themselves analyzed, so that they should be aware of their own biases before practicing; the same does not obtain in the student evaluation code. Yet, if you say that a certain teacher is poor, and your nearest educational authority assures you from the sidelines that your word goes, you have the obligation to know what good teaching is. What is good teaching? Making an abstruse subject lucid to a dolt? All too often it is simply making it entertaining rather than rigorous. "Demands for student participation conceal," writes Kingsley Amis, "a simple desire to have less studying to do, less of everything that relates in any way to studying."

In practice, what has happened by encouraging students to evaluate teachers has not been encouraging at all. Let us leave on one side the well-documented cases of reprisals taken by students on unpopular, or tough, teachers. In our case we found most students so busy, usually carrying some job on the side, that they had little time and even less inclination to sit on the various evaluative committees opened up to them. Those who had were the fanatics. It was like the shop steward system: only the political activist in the factory would give up time to serve. Furthermore, of course, the students are changing all the time. What one graduating class considered a valued quality, the next held to be anathema, and so on. We now learn that both sides of the sandwich in which faculty finds itself are fugitive, college presidents currently turning over with the rapidity of a student generation. Students all no doubt have the vote, but judging a political program that hasn't happened is quite different from passing opinion on a body of knowledge, a canon of texts, that has.

The egalitarian urge has thus further politicized the university in this area, giving politics, especially the subjective judging of men and women teachers, a new and arresting authenticity, and once again remaking the college in the model of the democracy beyond its walls that it can never be. Student evaluations have strengthened the administration and weakened the faculty, one increasingly reluctant to go against student opinion.

With typical irony this urge has had one illiberal outcome. By asking students to see a political power game in the university triad, you invite them, in the name of the taxpayer, to cut down authority. But any ordering of work is authoritative. The result? You destroy the liberal arts, in which everyone's say is now equal and each is entitled to his or her "interp." With the same stroke you revere science, which is *not* a series of interps and presents, in fact, the most authoritarian truths of the lot. For science is what it is (and what it is, Daniel Bell has written, "is a self-corrective system of disposing of useless facts"). Once again, the liberal educator takes up his Lincolnesque stance; he looks as if he is reforming society, emancipating the young, when he is really enchaining them for the promised Eldorado of science and technology, one that has polluted and poisoned our world.

When all the arguments are in, one realizes with a sense of shock that nothing rational has been said for student evaluation of faculty. On the contrary, everything rational has been said *against* the innovation—and you can't keep on writing off minds as keen as Jacques Barzun's as biased. In the words of CUNY's Robert Hoffman, "The activity of a teacher is to be specified by its correlative, the activity of a pupil. And a pupil is not just any learner, but a learner who learns by being taught."

Then, scratching one's head as to why none of these arguments and articles ever seems to have stopped the march toward more and more student governance in our public colleges, one realizes that in this sector you are not dealing with reason but emotion. Indeed, with religion. These earnest, flabby-faced men with their pince-nez and pot-bellies placed behind board-of-education desks are, as remarked, missionaries. This time they are not bringing Christianity to the poor aborigine; they are bringing EDUCATION. Their gospel in fact reverses religion, in which God becomes man, for under its aegis man becomes God; or should we say that the student becomes God, with a fervor unmatched anywhere else in the world? I shall pursue this point later. Let it merely be remarked here that our Catholic colleges, where presumably a higher authority than man is accepted, have permitted very few of these pressures to exercise much sway—with one or two atypical exceptions at Notre Dame. Let it lastly be added that the demotion of the teacher is not unconnected with the fact that during the 1970s assaults on teachers in New York City increased 77.4%, robberies of teachers by students by almost half as much.

It seems to me entirely conceivable that, by the time these words are being read, New York City will have institutionalized evaluation by *only* the most retarded ("disadvantaged") students. Why not? Of what worth is it to have a student evaluation of a Math professor by a young genius like Bobby Fisher? The "ghetto kids" are the ones who count. So, in order to make ourselves yet holier, let us proceed further into disadvantage and say that only Black ghetto kids should evaluate; after all, if a teacher has succeeded in making a subject clear and entertaining to them, he has succeeded. He has done his job. From that point of view it would be logical to refine standards further and require student evaluations to be performed only by Black ghetto female freshpersons. Then by gay Black ghetto, etc., and so on, down (or up) the line. The moral level of such possibilities soars, or recedes, almost out of sight. But of course we are not dealing with anything approaching logic. We are ending education.

A Trial of Force

3
The Riots

It was not a very difficult task, nor one requiring much courage, to "overthrow" a university, which is scarcely set up like an army camp. Dumping library cards takes about as much guts as tossing frisbees. Erasmus and More (who requested disemboweling and quartering rather than the axe) were braver. Indeed, "when one takes a truly courageous position," writes John Searle, "and defends the right of one's colleagues and students not to have their classes disrupted by left-wing activists, this is regarded as taking the easy way out, as selling out to the establishment, or worse." The one-way freedom proceeds apace.

Once again, student protest seemed on the surface liberally anti-authoritarian. "Never mind," Jacques Barzun reports overhearing in a reply to a canvasser for signatures to something or other on his campus; "if it's a protest, I'll sign it." With a democracy believing in numbers and with more people in America going to college than went in the whole world during the last century, something seemed surely wrong when, in the sixties, the young turned to disruption and hooliganism despite all the liberal values showered upon them. The note of pained surprise of J. Bronowski at this time, trustee of the Salk Institute for Biological Studies in San Diego, California, personifies the general dismay:

> A whole generation of liberals and humanists, to which I belong, is bewildered at the discovery that the young include us in their charge of hypocrisy. We made liberalism respectable by our labors, and turned it into an intellectual faith; and now we are distressed to find that our heroic memories of the hungry thirties and the Spanish Civil War are dismissed as an out-of-date mythology.

In their book *Passion and Politics: Student Activism in America*, Seymour Lipset and Gerald Schaflander review cases of campus unrest in America dating back to the beginning of the nineteenth century, but in no case does the element of surprise seem as considerable as it clearly was in the nineteen sixties. In *What Went Wrong with American Education* Peter Witonski put it as follows:

> We simply were not prepared for the kind of rampant Know-Nothingism that has reduced several of our major universities to states of near anarchy. Incredulous adults cannot understand why this most privileged generation of students should have chosen to behave in such a despicable manner. Older people who had to work and struggle to get through college are sickened and revolted by the stories of campus violence, and are hard pressed to find anything about the student radicals with which to be sympathetic.

This is another operative statement. It was the popular *incredulity* off which the media fattened; the campus disturbances of the sixties found the media ready to give them mass dissemination, free. This was far less the case, at first, in France, though later—in Japan, Holland, and, above all, West Germany—that is, the more prosperous countries—the American virus took root and the American student riot became the emulated pattern since it was one designed for exploitation by the media. Young Leroi stood on a corner of

125th Street after a class one evening, hectoring a group of five of his friends, a stringer for the *New York Times* among them; the next evening he found himself talking, rather more loudly, to ten of his friends and twenty media men. He mounted a packing case. The following night he was a student leader.

This was literally what happened in the only disturbance (if such it could be called) of this period that Oxford ever knew. Since England was not involved in the war in Vietnam, and had no civil rights issue to write home about, it was hard for even visiting American activists there to whip up trouble. But the BBC, which had been showing campus buildings burning right, left, and center in America, had to find some dissent on the home front and interviewed exactly ten students who had boldly demonstrated in front of the Bodleian Library on a deserted Bank Holiday in 1968. Subsequently, the Marcuse Society decided that All Souls College, which has no undergraduates, was fascistic and picketed it briefly, only to be seen off by the Fellows in residence.

It is true that a few red-brick universities in Britain later knew slightly more serious disturbances—notably Hull and Essex (whose brick is very red)—but thanks perhaps to the lack of need for a language filter, England was able to read American student rhetoric for what it was. This could more easily deceive Italians and Germans—indeed, the latter took it over verbatim. The leading Oxford activist of the sixties was a rich Pakistani called Tarik Ali. Prior to this period, in the relatively calm fifties, student protest was something that went on in Latin America, the stuff of farce. By the end of it, in Witonski's words, "It could be argued that every anti-American slogan used by the European left was first used by the American New Left." One could add that a principal feature of such rioting was that it should have no public support. This was a *sine qua non*. Outrage was what the media wanted.

A case has been made that the American academic citadel first began to betray itself, and crumble, by politicization in the fifties. In 1964-65 the catalytic Berkeley revolt took place, though it was by no means indigenous in inception; one of my former CCNY students appeared to be an original instigator. Abba Lerner, Professor of Economics at CUNY's Queens College, declared, "In Berkeley in 1964 Mario Savio discovered to his own and everybody else's surprise how easy it was to demoralize the faculty." Ironically enough, shortly before this Senator Barry Goldwater had been publicly assailed for purportedly being carried forward by student sentiment! Later, in Egypt, students were to rally and riot not for peace, but to get their government to go to war, thus dispelling the belief that the youth culture was axiomatically peaceful. For simply to be young guarantees little; at the time of the Beer Hall Putsch Hitler was only 34, Goering 30, and Himmler 23; on the other hand, the China that our young adulate today is politically a gerontology, with Mao 82, Chou En-lai 77, and four of the twenty-one members of the Politburo over eighty, most being over seventy.

It soon became questionable whether our ensuing riots were commanding of local student, let alone public, support. As John Coyne put it in *The Kumquat Statement*, "A great number of the flower children are over thirty." He had in mind Jerry Rubin and Abbie Hoffman, the former speaking at Kent State shortly before outside agitators converged on that campus and triggered the bloodbath. Moreover, a large number of these "student" revolutionaries were extremely peripheral students, at best. Mario Savio was marginal, as were Daniel Cohn-Bendit (a media creation if ever there was one) and Rudi Dutschke. Tarik Ali, who claimed at one point to represent the British undergraduate population, was not a student at all. At the time of the CCNY riots, discussed below, the editor of our most insurrectionary student newspaper had been jogging along in the freshman class for some eight or nine years.

However, if 2% of a student body could, as it found it could, bring a large university to a standstill, there was surely something wrong with the state of Denmark. Besides, there were blatant injustices abroad in the land. First the civil rights struggle, then the Vietnam "commitment." Even though almost all universities were on the side of the angels in both causes, activists managed to tie their actions to the coattails of each. *Saturday Review* liberals and the peace matrons went along for a while, making excuse after excuse for the publicized anarchy, until given a few hard kicks in the teeth by their Black brothers. CORE (Congress of Racial Equality), originally pacific, tossed out any Whiteys in its ranks and embraced violent methods of achieving its aims. SNCC or SNICK (Student Non-Violent Coordinating Committee), founded in 1961, also purged itself of Whites, Stokeley Carmichael succeeding, in May 1966, to the chairmanship (after such relative moderates as James Forman and John Lewis) and then himself ceding to H. Rap Brown; the organization finally, in Witonski's words, "survived a little longer as a kind of Non-Student Violent Coordinating Committee, advocating anti-Semitism, pan-Africanism, urban guerilla warfare, and Castroism." In other words, the UN standards of the mid-seventies. In 1967 the Panthers were started by Huey Newton and Bobby Seale, and the complexion, in all senses, of student revolt began to change.

Furthermore, a characteristic of American student riots was that they took place *in a period of massive support of education by government.* If the American university wanted to immolate itself publicly, it could scarcely have chosen a better moment. It is true that rioting took place at private institutions, even at a small college like Rochester in 1964, then at Harvard and Princeton (though it is sometimes forgotten that Cornell, site of a spectacular take-over, is a land-grant college deeply in debt to federal funding); but these generally followed outbreaks of violence at large, urban, tax-supported colleges. Student America bit the hand that fed it with a vengeance. Not that their self-elected, now-forgotten, leaders seemed to care. At Columbia Mark Rudd was cynically open about the lack of reason for his rebellion. "Let me tell you," he said, "we manufactured the issues. The Institute for Defense Analysis is nothing at Columbia. Just three professors. And the gym issue is bull. It doesn't mean anything to anybody. I had never been to the gym site before the demonstration began. I didn't even know how to get there."* Cohn-Bendit was to echo him in France: "First we must have a revolution. Then we can start talking about goals."

Needless to say, this "theory" was parroted by Norman Mailer in a *Harper's* article, where we were told that "you created the revolution first and learned from it, learned of what your revolution might consist and where it might go. . ." Unlike the traditional Marxist analysis, which preceded action, the New Left created "a revolution which preceded ideology." Your program supposedly arose out of what action was taken as you went along. To think that living trees were felled to print this rubbish! Had none of these hotheads ever made the acquaintance of Turgenev's Bazarov?

Elite ideologues like Mailer and Régis Debray, with their "comradeship of the fighting front" and "thinking with the

---

*Despite this statement SDS Harvard Senior Michael Kazin could still write, in 1969, "at Columbia the infamous gymnasium was the issue." The **old** gymnasium was what was infamous. In 1976 Columbia students picketed the gym to protest allowing neighborhood groups to use it!

blood," present what Martin Oppenheimer, in *The Urban Guerrilla*, calls "a strange alliance between humanistic politics and the worship of those less rational bases of politics which have traditionally been the source of support for . . . fascism." It is comforting to reflect that few of my present students have ever heard of either "thinker." But the gnostic nonideology was there in 1968, the year in which a New York City detective, who had infiltrated a Black nationalist group, testified that he had become part of a terrorist cell out to kill moderate civil rights leaders. "In short," writes Oppenheimer, "it was not freedom of speech that brought the Nazis to power—it was freedom to perform illegal acts of subversion without significant punishment."

Oddly enough, an aspect of this romance is a bureaucratic behavior common to both sorts of insurrection. Our revolting students were forever setting up cells, committees, defense groups, "paragovernments" and the rest of the abracadabra of cloud-cuckoo-land. In his *The Year of the Young Rebels* Stephen Spender observed this: "One of the paradoxes about the present generation of students who rebel against bureaucracy is that they themselves so often appear to be frustrated bureaucrats. The first thing they set up is a committee; the next, an office with telephones, typewriters, etc." For, if you have no theoretic program, only "thinking with the blood" and destruction now, you compensate by erecting a lot of apparatus that suggests you are really brimful of ideas; in fact, your theory is the bullhorn, and freedom of speech for nihilists only. The suicidal nature of the mission is aptly summarized by Spender when he writes: "Students who attempt to revolutionise society by first destroying the university are like an army which begins a war by wrecking its own base." Arthur Bestor's analogy for the same exercise is equally well put; he describes it as similar to "the bulldozing of cropland for an airfield as a form of agricultural improvement."

The most serious, and consequential, student riots of the sixties were the Sorbonne-Nanterre disturbances in 1968, which touched off a general strike and very nearly toppled a government. My wife and I were living in France on sabbatical at the time and, however the media may designate the direction of these events today, the fact is that these students struck out first and foremost for a better education; the matter began, at least, as very much a university affair. It is for this reason that it deserves to be called serious; intellectually it was so.

One could not help but feel sympathy for students who had one library seat per hundred and literally could not scramble into window-spots at lectures essential for their degrees. How spoiled their American counterparts seemed by comparison and, in particular, what spoiled babies those who paid nothing for tuition. These French lectures were droned-out, dismal affairs given by absurdly underpaid academics, a lot of them selling insurance and real estate on the side, so that the strike really began in their interest too. In America bad teaching was never at issue. Rochester, Berkeley, Columbia, Cornell, and Harvard had some of the finest teachers anywhere. So, we once liked to think, did CCNY. All were hotbeds of unrest, of strictly political rather than pedagogical happenings.

In France the Communist strength among teachers—certainly among *lycée* teachers—owes considerably to such poor payment, and it was a feature of the first demonstrations at the Nanterre campus of the Sorbonne that the Communists beat up student marchers as lustily as Wall Street construction workers would later deal with their American counterparts. French Communists, ably assisted by their powerful union the CGT, were doing very well thank-you through the parliamentary process. *L'Humanité* excoriated the students from the start.

Fanatic factions then began within the student ranks, some of which Cohn-Bendit, neither a Frenchman nor a true student, corralled opportunistically into politics. Yet still these young people occupied themselves principally at the gates of academe, where their graffiti, incidentally, were of a wit and intelligence seldom seen in America. It was hard not to feel some affection for these French youths, more especially since French *flics* were bashing in the heads of their professors beside them. Then the Renault workers came out, and the tumbrils started to roll.

In America both the first Berkeley and Columbia riots, and those at ("It couldn't happen here") Harvard were sociopolitical in direction. Columbia became the model for the latter part of the decade, and beyond it, generally owing to that university's proximity to the media. The destructive Moses Hall riot at Berkeley was, according to one professor who watched it, "modeled frankly on Columbia." To see Mark Rudd perched in his president's swivel chair, jauntily puffing at his president's cigars, while his cohorts sorted through private papers for proof of tie-ins with that ubiquitous demon, "the military-industrial complex," was the kind of gorgeously theatrical affront on which television thrives. It was more real—McLuhan would say "reel"—than reality.

For never was McLuhan's narcissus-narcosis theory (we mesmerize ourselves in mirrors) better exemplified than in those days: faculty members seeing pictures of themselves standing guard at Widener Library; Blacks with rifles at Cornell. I remember riding one morning subway filled with New York high school students who had been imported to disrupt our campus the day before, and who, I surmised, were on their way to more of the same. They were excitedly, laughingly, passing around a copy of that day's *Daily News* in which appeared pictures of themselves trashing some building—"Hey, there's Earl. . .an' ain' dat Dook?" They were delighted at the mirror image. Eventually we all got out and I walked up the hill beside them, I to teach, they to trash. Presently the student center's public address system would announce, "Professor X's class is still in progress. Would somebody please go over and disrupt it?" A colleague on Fulbright in Holland at the time saw our Aronow Auditorium ablaze on the television screen. I am not sure that he was not closer to the essence of what was going on than those of us who stood and watched it; in New York a camera crew could be drummed up in minutes.

Ostensibly, the first stirrings at Columbia owed to a grave concern for Morningside Park and its abused tenants of junkies and pushers; for the university threatened to encroach a few yards into the rock face and erect a gym. Arrangements were being made for members of the community and others to enjoy this gym at stated times. Anyone who ever used what was Columbia's old gym, walking down several flights from the so-called locker room to the so-called swimming pool and bumping into weight-lifters, fencers, runners, and so forth en route, knew that Lions were getting a shoddy shake for their money in comparison with almost any other private college. At that time Columbia had one so-called squash court; Harvard had forty-eight. But Columbia's gym issue was the People's Park for Berkeley.

In the event, the gym running into the park was not built; the university has now constructed one entirely on its own grounds, to which, of course, the public are not allowed access. The point is that the protest was not really an academic so much as a social outcry, and it set the American pattern to come. When our own President took office a few years ago, his first communication to the faculty had nothing to do with academic matters, but concerned the ratio of minority workers on a nearby building site over which, it transpired, the college had no control in any case. This political righteousness coupled with uncertainty of office was by and large the norm. One college president so lost confidence in his role that he took a sabbatical off as a construction worker. He even wrote a book about it. Twenty years ago nothing more ludicrous could have been conjectured.

With the stepping up of the Vietnam war by President Johnson, student protest turned almost entirely political in America, on the basis of two wrongs making a right, or, as John Searle put it, "because the war and racism are so dreadful, it is acceptable and indeed justifiable to engage in further irrational and malicious behavior, however remote this behavior may be from having any effect on either." I gave a first faculty talk against involvement in our Finley Ballroom, years before others were taking it seriously or finding it fashionable, and I sat in at our first sit-in of the Administration Building (the only other teacher I saw there that night was Eric Bentley, from Columbia). By the end of the sixties any campus that had *not* had a disruption didn't rate. The front page of the *New York Times* began to look like campaign coverage of a running war—Chicago bombed, Wayne State burnt, sit-ins at Syracuse, Cleveland, New Mexico State; then McNamara's 1969 visit to Harvard, and the deaths of students at Kent and Jackson State. The spring of 1968 saw some form of campus unrest at over half the nation's colleges, including more than two hundred cases of arson. Over 55% of these disruptions occurring between 1968 and 1970 were related to racial problems in the society at large, not unique to America, to be sure, but more her problem than Europe's.

The academic side of student unrest began to get fairly fatuous. By the end of the decade every possible "non-negotiable demand" had been sent in, including one that thudded into my mailbox requiring a guaranteed $25,000-a-year job for every graduate. Meanwhile, the internecine

squabblings and bickerings of the various student sects grew
rococo enough to be worthy of some gay party; Michael Kazin,
SDS Harvard, tells us:

> At the 1969 national convention in Chicago, S.D.S. expelled the
> members of the Progressive Labor Party from the organization.
> The P.L.P., a pro-Chinese Marxist-Leninist party, was charged
> with opposing most of the demands and actions of the Black
> liberation movement, including the key one of "self-determina-
> tion" for Afro-Americans; was accused of slandering maliciously
> in its official publications the positions of the Black Panther Party
> (with which the S.D.S. has a close fraternal relationship); and was
> chastised for many of its international positions, including
> labeling the leadership of the Vietnamese revolution "traitors" for
> entering into the Paris negotiations. . . . P.L.P. derided its
> expulsion and continued to meet in the convention hall, proclaim-
> ing itself the "legitimate S.D.S."

Any form of reality was soon lost sight of (far from the
case at Nanterre); to gain attention in multi-media America
you had to be extreme, and to be exteme you had to be more
and more irrational. You had to talk about near-bankrupt
colleges as having political power. The loose Oxbridge format
of old was almost risibly "permissive," and I think any Oxford
or Cambridge undergraduate of either sex, circa 1938, would
have been utterly baffled to read an SDS exhortation
(courtesy, this time, Carl Davidson) of the late sixties, that
"the purpose of desanctification is to strip institutions of their
legitimizing authority, to have them reveal themselves to the
people under them for what they are—raw coercive power."

In America this surrealism was further exacerbated by
the effort to try to force the academe into a labor-management
grid. Such rarely occurred elsewhere, as the flames of
campus unrest spread to Japan, India, and (one of the worst
sites) West Berlin, where teaching was brought to a standstill.
The irony was that while students, and their odious little
toadies among the faculty, were supposed to be "workers,"

with administration and faculty "management," the agitators often seemed incensed by the genuine bond forged between faculty unions and labor.

By now the chips are in. It was a Black, Bayard Rustin, who convincingly demonstrated that integration has been furthered, rather than retarded, by the common labor cause. The utopian attempt of Black Power militants at this time, Rustin has shown, to effect a viable bridge between liberal intellectuals and a handful of semi-criminal fanatics did irreparable damage to the Black cause and set back the genuine advances won on the labor front, often through unionization.

So the tragic farce of bombs and burnings went on. People peacefully studying in libraries or laboratories (as at the University of Wisconsin) were murdered by stray bullets and bombs. And what rotten shots most of these morons were; they couldn't even hit John Bunzel, the highly conspicuous President of California State at San Jose, with a bomb. Everything got done as the Yahoos awaited the coming of the cameras, then clenched their fists, chanted their slogans—"Right on!. . .Pigs!. . .Fuzz!"—until enough footage had been obtained and the CBS vans could drive off, contented. One president even had dung smeared on his door. It was notable, too, that it was always in spring, the first of the sunny weather, that the liberal conscience awakened, like Dostoevsky's character who had to time his feelings for humanity to Tuesdays. Camera crews can't get good shots inside dark crowded corridors and classrooms, what with all those beards. So ours was a running Easter Story. Our terms were set back earlier and earlier, by a shaky Registrar, so that you could finish classes before the busts began.

"Hey, son," said smiling Dad, in many a living-room of that era, "where d'you think you're going with all those Peace and Love signs?"

"Huh? Oh, just to burn down the Admin Building like and picket a bank like and shoot up a few pigs an'. . . ."

"Fine. Just so long as you're really *with it*, son.''

"Let it all hang out, man," called Sis, from the set.

"Heavy."

Apparently the flower children are today on skid row. A 1974 University of California survey of "street people" on Berkeley's Telegraph Avenue found a population of former university hippies leading a life of fruitless fantasy on sidewalks, selling their blood to buy marijuana joints and cheap wine and doze off long afternoons in the sun. To such has the liberal ethic, allowing anything so long as it is anti-American, lured its Gadarene herd of "disadvantaged."

By 1970, the year of the Cambodian invasion, three out of ten university undergraduates wanted to live elsewhere than in the U.S. of A., while civil disobedience had become a minor academic requirement, with Martin Luther King virtually sainted, like trashing the ROTC. In the latter instance we at CCNY, where the President "heartily endorsed" ROTC's ouster, were treated to a bizarre reversal; after our pathetic little handful of ROTC students were forced off campus, and the program stopped, a Black coed wrote in to the student newspaper infuriated that she had been denied the possibility of such courses involving rifle-range practice. ROTC had been helping her to learn how to gun down Whitey.

By now reams, small libraries, have been written on these student riots, and I must confess to having committed some of this pseudo-sociology myself—understanding infantilism, like picking at a scab, exerts a strange fascination. But that was in another country and, besides, the wench is dead. The mayhem that took place on our campus where "goon-squads" (the term is the well-chosen one of our Acting President) of roving Blacks out of Harlem beat up Jewish girls on their way to class, and then found their obscenities interpreted as a mandate for open admissions by a craven administration, has been the subject of an admirable book by Louis Heller. Indeed, the jacket put on our then President Buell Gallagher's account of these times, *Campus in Crisis*, neatly summarizes the whole: against a garishly red background (the flames of hell?) one of our buildings is seen burning down. A grinning coed, no doubt bra-less, to left. A media man, gear slung about him, to right. Center stage, ignored by camera and sound men, we see a sweating fire department crew risking their necks to put out the needless blaze, when they might surely have been engaged on more serious errands elsewhere. Our damage was in the millions. Imagine what national collegiate destruction amounted to during this period. It has probably been estimated somewhere.

Heller's book, *The Death of the American University*, is sound and should be required· reading for educational administrators; but it is much too mild in its exegesis of what went on at City College in the spring of 1969. The spring *putsch* that year was sheer Evelyn Waugh, with its spectacle of an ordained minister as President "negotiating" with a self-declared nonentity calling itself "the Black and Puerto Rican student community," playing on his faculty (as one eminent professor put it) "like a harp," and finally being served with a number of writs to reopen, one handled by the city Comptroller and Mayoral aspirant, Mario Procaccino. The only trouble with this picture was that some 28,000 other students, mostly Jewish, happened to be on the dirtier end of this stick, or *schtick*.

From the start Gallagher gloried in having his presidential face rubbed in the dirt, a task effected with regularity throughout the year by the pro-SDS college paper, which had earlier done its best to rally support for an Army deserter on campus; but the main mass of students remained unmoved by this confectioned *casus belli*, even when cruel cops hauled the youth off and Dean of Students Jim Peace [*sic*] was undemocratic enough to prefer charges against the handful of little Hitlers who had vandalized his premises and intimidated his secretary. For this and other sanities Jim Peace was censured by the faculty and later resigned.

The Gallagher story is another book, but it contributes to this one since its symptomatology reveals the liberal death wish in an advanced condition. Here was this Christian minister and civil rights advocate suddenly confronted by a group of Blacks raging against him. As he convened his faculty into Great Hall and stood on the podium in front of a mural of Alma Mater presenting a diploma, the place was invaded by absurdly armed militants whose leader (a youth who had scarcely been to class all term) took over the platform and snarled foul profanities at his President. The minister paled but waved back those faculty who rose to his assistance, saying—"It's all right." It was the most pathetic spectacle I have seen in my life. Apparently, in the endless "negotiation" that ensued with these militants, they virtually gave up on their demands and simply went on steadily cursing Buell Gallagher, "who sat head down throughout the transactions, not replying at all." Clearly he saw himself as Christ, taking on himself the sins of this world.

One rainy April morning I found an exceedingly polite Black youth of about sixteen installing a mattress in my office. When I asked him what he thought he was doing, he looked at a list in his hand, "This is 918, isn't it?" I nodded and, with a last look to see that the bedding was in order, he left. That afternoon our South Campus, once a convent (so far Waugh would not have had to alter a word of the script), was firmly closed, by *Black Mischief*, with stout chains. To at least one eye that bedraggled bunch, waving their home-made Vietcong flags and chanting "Pow-err to de Peepul," looked like a belated blackface act, in whose ranks, incidentally, I searched in vain for any Puerto Ricans.

For about ten minutes a platoon of bored police stared the raggle-taggle mob in the face disbelievingly, and then mooched off. Professor Morris Silver, Chairman of the Economics Department, proposed that we forcibly reopen those gates in the name of the taxpayer, but he received little support. Gallagher had decided not to be Hayakawa. In fact, the man who had gone so courageously after the Communists in our ranks in the McCarthy era was to say that, rather than call the cops, "I would submit to the rule of law by going to jail." *Quod erat* something or other.

After nearly two weeks' occupation, the New York Board of Higher Education, acting (for once) under popular pressure, ordered the institution reopened and, with a restraining order signed by a State Supreme Court Justice on the way, the rebels fled. Their incumbency had been marked by a movement of our North Campus School of Engineering to reopen (aborted by Gallagher), an ignored UCRA faculty ballot to do the same, and the usual antics of SDS trying to get in on the act by "seizing" a deserted and very seizable small brick building, which they rechristened after the latest Black to have killed a cop. Once more, as at Columbia, the SDS were first to run, their coats drawn over their faces.

The taxpayers, therefore, got the college open on Tuesday, May 6th. Wednesday was worse than ever. The now customary troop of SDS invaded my morning classes (though not that one held at 8 A.M.), were made intellectual mincemeat of by their peers in the question period I managed to insinuate into their harangue, and escaped in some disorder. Seeing that the discredited SDS were getting nowhere, their rallies turning into yawning matches, the hard core got busy with rocks and chairs through windows, and metal pipes and clubs on the campus outside. Professors had fire extinguishers opened in their faces, women were thrown down concrete stairs, fires were started in buildings and the Emergency Room of the nearby Knickerbocker Hospital looked like a Casualty Clearing Station of World War Two. The best of us bloodied some noses—I recall a burly ex-Harvard Classics Professor, who had just completed a class on Thucydides, flooring a leading militant and smashing his silly shades—but it was not fair fighting. Brave Black boys were clubbing girls. At least three coeds in my own classes had to be escorted to Knickerbocker. On Thursday the cops were called, after more brawling and head-opening, and arrests were made, including the anticipated quorum of local lads whose sole connection with the college seemed to be the possession of a Molotov cocktail, doubtless devised thanks to the instructions for such given by the *New York Review of Books.* By Friday Gallagher had had enough. Having resigned six (or was it seven?) times, he resigned; a Biology Professor, Joseph Copeland, was appointed Interim President.

With the cessation of thuggery, and the college ceasing to shut every now and then like some spastic rat-trap, a certain clearing of the air was felt and a real solidarity with one's more serious students. By this time everyone had been called racist, including our Kenneth Clark, so the term had become useless as an insult and generally turned into something closer to "thinker." The demands of the militants began to be examined more calmly, one trouble being that they weren't written in English and another that it was by no means clear whom we were dealing with; our faculty elected three spokesmen but the other side seemed to have a fluid bunch of "representatives," the more constant of whom appeared not to be students at all, but very tense SEEK (Search for Education Elevation Knowledge) teachers, some of them already fired. The chief demand was for open admissions and, as we shall see in a subsequent section, here peace was bought at any price.

Weak administration policies, then as now, proved both costly and useless. At CCNY we saw a craven collapse in the face of violence on the part of our President, plus a capitulation to a tiny group of foul-mouthed enrolees with whom there should never have been any negotiation. Obscenities were heaped on Buell Gallagher and the more they were, the more he smiled behind his steel-rimmed spectacles. Only occasionally, in those confrontations in Great Hall, could a red flush be seen creeping up his neck, to emerge verbally, with astonishing venom, as he reproved a faculty member in the catchphrase *paternalistic!*

Our latest president to date came from the Physics Department of Rochester University, where I had had the benefit of his acquaintance at occasional luncheons. He came trailing clouds of glory from the first atom-bomb project. Rumored to have been chosen for his extreme sympathy to students, he instantly instituted a Black Studies Department, with total Black faculty (presumably on the principle that only a plant can teach botany), created a Black Vice President, firing—so it was reputably alleged—a White Jewish Dean, and earning his new laurels by providing funds to send a group of Black students to the National Black Political Convention in Gary, Indiana.

All this to no effect. At last reading our Black student newspaper (entitled *The Paper*) was continuing to editorialize vehemently against him, writing an "Open Letter" in the spring of 1974 accusing poor Marshak, of all people, of infringing affirmative-action directives. At Ohio University at this time President Claude R. Sowle, another young liberal who had initiated student-faculty participation in policy-making, confessed that Athens activists had taken advantage of such "openness." Pelted with bottles and physically jostled, he too gave in and resigned, thus joining that distinguished frieze of departed presidents, including Princeton's Goheen and Cornell's Perkins.

Almost alone, S. I. ("Don") Hayakawa opposed the hooligans at this time. In this case, it was San Francisco State. Significantly he was, like CCNY's Louis Heller, a semanticist. Such men had become too familiar with verbal duplicity to be easily deceived (it was Columbia's Amitai Etzioni who remarked that if someone insulted you, it was poor communication not to show you were insulted back). Don Hayakawa wrote me in a moving letter, typical of his dedication: "The situation at SF State is cool and beautiful. No cops on campus (we never did have the National Guard) and tranquillity for fourteen months or so. No repression. Only firm action against criminal acts (which the New Left *calls* repression). Works just fine."

Above all, Don did not buy the idea of permanent rebellion as some sort of educative experience. A Columbia sophomore of 1968 vintage looks back on the latter in a best-selling paperback, later, naturally enough, made into a movie; *The Strawberry Statement* contains the following solemn *aperçu*: "Kids are much less uptight about breaking rules that they have been taught not to break. For example, during the strike, I had great misgivings about breaking down a door. Now I wouldn't." So when bricks were hurled into his office, Don Hayakawa flung the bricks back. He never called the National Guard and he kept his campus open and operating for the majority of students who wanted to continue going to class and to graduate. He worked on the principle: Do unto the SDS what they would do unto you, only *do it first*, taunting and gibing at SDS from the stage when they heckled him, as in one famous instance at Colorado University where his hecklers walked right into two-year prison sentences. How different from Cornell's President Perkins, who told faculty members that they "could not use the cloak of academic freedom to cover up statements which might anger black students." At the end of that particular term I said to a colleague, "Well, Don won." The shocked response I received was, "Think of the scars left on that institution." Who started the scarring? Hey, Officer, his jaw hit my fist. In one instance at our college an infuriated Black, incensed at being denied the ability to go to class by a small group of radicals, actually broke into a building they had seized. One could understand his anger.

Capitulation is never a remedy. But despite the lessons of Columbia and Cornell (where not only the President but a Dean condemned a professor's claims for Western civilization as racism) and CCNY, it went on and on. For a while our Interim President Joseph Copeland, a wise and humane biologist, a man who had adopted Black children and headed the prestigious Asa Wright Foundation north of Arima in Trinidad, stopped the rot; he knew that a small "student" faction, alien to the scholarly community, threatened the very life of the institution, contemptuous of academic and other liberties and claiming to impose the values of "action."

But Copeland left, and the ostrich policy began again under his successor. The result was that by listening to the (almost daily altered) demands as the taxpayers' mandate, our administration effectively destroyed what our college had stood for during a century; it lowered abysmally the worth of its degree, and left its faculty in disorder and dismay. So divided was our History Department, where a stalwart few refused to concede all standards, that it was openly stigmatized on the front page of the *New York Times* as a "political cesspool." Here pugilism practically became an academic qualification. When a young woman activist slugged Professor Stanley Page in the face, nothing happened; she retired for a while to Sarah Lawrence (where else?) and was gently promoted *in absentia*.

The ostrich policy persists as if by some inner necessity, some biological urge. It is only very occasionally that such administrators are brought to book by their students and faculty, or that a university (like George Washington) actually expels students who seize buildings. It is therefore refreshing to record the case, not only of San Francisco State (where the average age of students was between twenty-five and twenty-six) under Hayakawa, but also of the University of Toronto in 1974.

Early in March of that year about twenty Toronto radicals began making life unusually unbearable for speakers like Edward Banfield of the University of Pennsylvania (who was only saved from physical injury by last-minute intervention by students and faculty) and for those of their professors they disliked, insulting and harassing them in classroom and on street alike. A delegation to the President, John Evans, did no good, despite its backing of student signatures for the disciplining of this largely SDS-led group. However, the Faculty Association of Toronto made its own firm demand, that the administration restore order, and they made it stick; the radical ringleaders were soon learning democracy the hard way, in the courts. Ironically enough, the president began to receive praise in the press for his vigorous stand!

The psychopathology of academic dissidence in recent years deserves serious study. There is definitely some sixth or seventh sense at work here. The extremist sniffs out the martyr with the sure nose of a beagle for a cringing hare. The capitulator is always the first casualty. Gallagher was ours, close followed by then CUNY Chancellor Albert Bowker, like

Gallagher another recurrent resigner who somehow seemed still to be in power each time the smoke cleared; Bowker took much credit for the open admissions program (to deafening applause from the *New York Times*). But he too turned in his tags and wisely departed for the West, where he can still be heard from, booming away about the beauties of open admissions while his faculties try to pick up the mess.

Directly one administrator is discredited, another Pied Piper appears ready to take his place and be carried off to the guillotine in turn, mouthing last speeches about moral duty and academic freedom. Equally, the activist stays clear of anyone who stands really firm, and looks likely, like Don Hayakawa, to give him a black eye in the bargain—those, in particular, who refuse to have their arms tied behind their backs by the charge of racism.

The lack of reason in our reality—the Kennedy assassinations, then Watergate—sanctions the irrational in the dissident group. It has always seemed incredible to me that people who could write the stuff SDS put out, notably in their *New Left Notes*, were ever taken seriously at all. But the paranoid thriller is popular at the moment, and not only in fiction. Just as Stalin had to see a spy at every street corner, so our latest sectarian student groups are obsessed with "conspiracies," finding enemies in almost every one.

Early in 1974 the *New York Times* reported a new student group, loosely organized under a guru, called NCLC (National Caucus of Labor Committees), dedicated not only to beating up their opponents but also to torturing the "traitors" within their own ranks. Paul Montgomery of the *Times* tells how NCLC members "now spend their waking hours being harangued in violent speeches studded with accusations that their enemies are forcing them to eat excrement, perform fellatio on pigs and dogs, and submit to homosexual rape." Among such enemies are evidently the Russian KGB, the

British Intelligence Service, and the Anthropology Department of Columbia. *Measure* magazine published some of the writings—ravings?—of NCLC. They were almost unbelievable. No sooner was one young demagogue set up as the savior of the people than a few weeks later he, or she, was revealed as a treacherous lackey of the CIA, the FBI, or the New York City Police Department—or all three combined.

To testify further to the continuance of student radicalism, a new organization of young activists arose later in the year, advocating "total revolution" and calling itself MOVE. Education was now not even an aside. Founded by one John Africa, its premises were "based not on philosophy, not on theory, not on concepts, but doing away with those."

With a membership allegedly made up of ex-dope addicts, bank robbers, former American Nazis, as well as mere students and teachers, MOVE disrupted an appearance by Daniel Ellsberg at the University of Pennsylvania, forced the Chairwoman of the National Black Feminist Organization off the stage, and then proceeded to similar actions at innocent Temple University. But to date nothing very strenuous has been done to oppose the group. At last report Pennsylvania's Dean of Students, Alice Emerson, intended to "observe the situation." I well remember the then Chairman of my own department (now of course a college president) gravely asking us to consider what we ought to do if a new group, calling itself the Weathermen, decided to invade our classrooms. No one suggested chucking them out or, in the case of our more decrepit members, getting our guards to do so. One professor actually mooted the idea of incorporating the happening into the class, absorbing the riot by osmosis, as it were. Weeks later chairs and tables were sailing through our windows, etc.

The psychological instability of something like Tom Hayden's *Trial*, in which America appears to be a Fascist cauldron of terror and oppression, has by now been wildly surpassed in the literature and pathology of these new groups. But it was certainly this successful book, dealing with the events of one bloody summer in Chicago, 1968, that set some sort of model. "From now on," Hayden wrote, "even middle-class White children would no longer be safe from the paranoid wrath of the older, entrenched generation. We had seen it coming at the Pentagon, at Columbia, and in the streets of Chicago, and finally at People's Park, where murderous bullets were unleashed against tender white skin."

Hayden's Amerika crawls with FBI informers, special Justice Department "task forces" out to get you, police clubbing you down monotonously to chants of "Sieg Heil!"— "The thudding of fists and the screams of pain became part of the pattern of insanity." The pattern is prevalent, Judge Julius J. Hoffman being described, in one place, as a "madman." Only the Panthers are not insane. Representing perhaps about 0.1% of under 11% of the population, the Panthers are the ubiquitous and universal victims of repression, of a country that "is cracking down on those who want peace, racial solidarity, and self-determination." The poor Panthers (who certainly have shown little sign of desiring the first of these elements) "are no different from prisoners held in Santo Domingo, Saigon, or any other center of the American empire." But try to help them, Whitey, and you do so at your paternalistic peril:

> The slogan "Free Huey" must be enlarged to "Free All Political Prisoners." Many whites cling to the concept of a "fair trial" for the Panthers because they do not want to accept fully the idea of self-determination for blacks. This leads them to believe that they should examine the "facts" of Panther court cases before deciding to support the Panthers.

In short, you cannot win, nor are you intended to. Angela Davis was forever declaiming, before her own, that the only fair trial would be no trial—precisely what she might expect to receive in Russia, that is. In the event, her jury wined and dined her the evening of her acquittal. None of her posturing rhetoric helped her, however, with the Symbionese Liberation Army, which repudiated her violently. At one point in his diatribe Hayden informs us that "one Chicago psychiatrist told us of several cases in which police wives filed for divorce because their husbands would not even make love with them." If he can believe this, he can believe anything. The tragic paranoia of the fantasy world these activists created, and into which they lured others, attained a macabre funeral pyre in the flaming California house in which self-styled General Field-Marshal Cinque died surrounded by a weaponry that would have overequipped my whole platoon in the last war.

When Nelson Rockefeller suggested incorporating CUNY into SUNY, and imposing a small tuition fee on students, one of ours, a member of the Labor Committee wrote in our *Observation Post*:

> We are fighting the murderous capitalist class lead [*sic*] by mass murderer Nelson Rockefeller and the CIA to determine whether we will all live through the next two to five years. The bloody hand behind the truckers' violence, the layoffs in major industries, and the massive fuel and upcoming food shortages is Rockefeller's . . . These visible features of Rockefeller's plan for totalitarian governments make Adolf Hitler seem a quiet country gentleman.

Put beside this the invocation made (evidently from prison) by guru Timothy Leary, also gleefully printed by the same student newspaper (indirectly funded by the taxpayers) and you get the general atmosphere on our campus today:

> Brothers and Sisters, at this time let us have no more talk of peace . . . this is war for survival. Ask Huey and Angela. They dig it. . . . I declare that World War III is now being waged by short-haired robots whose deliberate aim is to destroy the complex web of free

wild life by the imposition of mechanical order. . . . Listen, Americans. Your government is an instrument of total lethal evil.

From the vantage point of the mid-seventies we may now try to assess something of the damage this *furor scholasticus* did, and pick up, as it were, a few of the bricks dropped by our predecessors. The sciences have been least harmed, since science is itself revolutionary. Oh, our college's Earth and Planetary Sciences Department was intemperately accused, only the other day, by three students of being "conservative," but this was a tempest in a teacup. It is when you move away from the empirical into the social or pseudo-sciences that activism of the rawer sort can still get its head, a Schockley or a Banfield be bravely shouted down, and rocks hurled. So-called student groups like CAR* (Committee Against Racism) and SDS continue to carry on in the old style, persecuting professors and disrupting their lectures and banning their books—SDS *New Left Notes* of early 1974 claiming to have "succeeded in banning *Introduction to Sociology* by John and Mavis Blezanz" for its "culture of poverty" theory.

In the spring of 1974, a decade after its triumphs, SDS contented itself with intimidating a fairly small group of professors and lecturers whom they felt they could smear with racism, including John Bunzel, already mentioned, Banfield, and men like Richard Herrnstein and Ellis Page, whom they chanted off the stage at San Francisco ("Hook and Page should be put in a cage"). Poor Banfield caught most of this fire, even more of it than Schockley, though his ration was less

---

*Surely the acronyms of the era also deserve study: a true acronym should form a word expressive of what the initials stand for, e.g. FAIR (Federated Associations for Impartial Review) or Valerie Solinas's SCUM (Society for Cutting Up Males). Compare, then, AAAAS (Association of African and Afro-American Students), so influential at Harvard during the events there of April 1969.

widely publicized. When he was invited to speak by the American Studies Committee at the University of Toronto, SDS sought to court even the local Italian community by "exposing" an allegedly anti-Latin book Banfield had written years ago, in fact a sympathetic study of an impoverished Italian village. Twelve hundred Toronto students later signed a petition calling for the disciplining of these disruptors.

There was a hint of desperation in these storm-troop tactics by SDS, an attempt to beef up their image in the face of rival factions, like NCLC perhaps. Thus when a CAR activist delivered an address at Wayne State at this time, after the scheduled speaker, Professor Lachman, had been shouted down, SDS complained that this was a waste of time "in private discussion with the professor while not being active in the class from the start." (Odd how one treasured those in the class who were "active" twenty years ago; today it means belligerent.) As SDS "targeted Banfield for exposure and harassment," it made up and sent out libelous flyers showing Hitler reading one of Banfield's books under "WANTED— DEAD OR ALIVE: EDWARD BANFIELD." Lionel Trilling had been the subject of a previous criminally WANTED poster treatment, as also our Interim President Copeland.

It would hardly seem reasonable to call sensible a spring of such excesses, during which the President of Ohio University was forced to resign to the accompaniment of flying bricks and gasoline flames, and Antioch College ("Brave and liberal little Antioch," as Buell Gallagher called it) once more shut down its campus; indeed, in the fifties this would have been turmoil.

But by the norms of the late sixties the nation's campuses were calm. This calm was variously described in the press, as "ominous," an "unquiet quiet," and the like. The Report of the Carnegie Commission of this year underlined the emphasis. If the campuses were quiet, something was surely seething under their surfaces. In 1971 some 45% of American college students felt America to be "a sick society." By 1974 this figure had dropped by 10%. Moral: if you don't hate America, that's apathy.

This is the first, but by no means least, of the damages done to the academy by the student violence of the sixties. It seems now assumed that if the university is functioning fairly normally—and the TANYA WE LOVE YOU notices were about the extent, in seriousness, of any dissent we at that time knew—then it is suffering from "apathy." You could have done well with an article for the *New York Times Magazine* at this moment, pointing out the absence of student unrest as diagnostic of another, even more shattering, bust to come. You could have quoted Irving Howe: "If, for instance, the deceits and inflated claims associated with 'open enrollment' in our university help evoke a backlash, we can expect that a decade later there will be still another and perhaps more serious version of the same policy."

Second, a dependency of the above, the reason why a lot of the big campuses like our own were quiet was not that SDS and their ilk were in ideological rags and tatters, but rather the reverse. Faculty SDS, from the President himself down, were in charge. True apathy was that expressed in a once-celebrated Princeton poll of the fifties, to which Aldous Huxley, among others, made concerned rejoinder in *Brave New World Revisited*. With the SDS or its mental equivalent in charge in a college, its shibboleths parroted by both faculty and students alike, forbidden knowledge takes on a curious reflection in Alice's fabulous looking-glass.

On one side, you forbid forbidden knowledge, stone Schockley, and "stop the presses on De Cecco" (SDS *New Left Notes*). As, bemused, and still persisting in believing in academic freedom despite the President of Cornell, you pass through the watery solid of Alice's mirror, you hear the *Wall Street Journal* lamenting the suppression of political satire in Yugoslavia—the Yugoslav government refused permission to Milovan Djilas and Mihajlo Mihajlov to attend the same San Francisco conference at which CAR denied the platform to Ellis Page—and then you meet a well-heeled fellow carrying a copy of the *New York Review of Books* that deplores the plight of dissident Marxist professors in Belgrade, while just behind him struts a contingent of our own AFL-CIO all ready to underwrite a lecture tour by Alexander Solzhenitsyn. There is a story told of Georg Lukàcs, the famous Hungarian Marxist literary critic: Lukàcs had long resisted recognition of the bourgeois Jew Kafka. When Russian thugs seized him and other professors and imprisoned him in a half-ruined castle, to treat him there with alternating bouts of brutality and bonhomie, Lukàcs is said to have conceded, "So Kafka was a realist after all, was he?" At City College he is alive and well.

Why shilly-shally any further? The SDS, both student and faculty, are performing the office, in a mirror image, of what Russia, and Greece, and Portugal, and Cuba, and China were doing at the time—denying free speech. They have denied it with success at several of the weaker links in our academic chain, principally those guilty of what Professor Marcuse calls, in a remarkable oxymoron, "repressive tolerance." It remains to be seen what may have been learned by these expensive lessons. Meanwhile, the sober Cox Commission's *Report on Crisis at Columbia* reminds us what they mean in terms of national life, in a country where education was for so long the very cornerstone of democracy: "The survival—literally the survival—of the free university depends upon the entire community's active rejection of disruptive demonstrations."

4
The Criminal as Hero

Pig professor or piggier student?

Let us listen for a moment to what the gurus of the time have been telling us:

> Should not every student develop a cultural paranoia in which every professor is viewed as a potential agent or tacit supporter of the murder factory and every academic system is seen as set against the student's mental and social health until he finds out differently? (Nat Hentoff, 1968)

> The American school system will be ended in two years. We are going to bring it down. Quit being students. Become criminals. We have to disrupt every institution and break every law. (Jerry Rubin, 1970)

The textbook before me, as I confronted my first class of open admissions students, was a thick one. It had been assigned me for a course in English composition; selflessly assembled for our use by our Chairman (now, of course, a Dean), it was a series of essays on "Cult Heroes of Our Time" entitled *Representative Men*.

I soon learnt that "our" time is not their time, though the book bore a 1970 copyright, the year in which Rubin urged students to become criminals and the year after Hentoff wanted *every* professor to be seen as a "tacit supporter of the murder factory" (despite the fact that thousands of professors were working for peace in Vietnam long before Hentoff was). There were essays on or by Arthur Schlesinger Jr., Marshall McLuhan, J. D. Salinger, Allen Ginsberg, Arthur Miller, Andy Warhol, Murray Gell-Mann, Jonas Salk, and John Paul Getty—men of whom none of my students had heard. An Introduction confidently assured us that "Salinger is the one American writer whose works most students know intimately," though none of mine knew of him at all. On the other hand, they did know something of other "representative men" (some of them women) represented, notably Malcolm X, Eldridge Cleaver, Martin Luther King, Sidney Poitier, Elizabeth Taylor, Timothy Leary, and Jacqueline Onassis. After all, only two weeks before we came to Timothy Leary, one of our student newspapers had published, apparently approvingly, his lengthy apologia for hijackings: "Remember the Sioux and the German Jews and the black slaves and the marijuana pogroms and the pious TWA indignation over airline hijackings. . . .Right on, Leila Khaled!"

An "Instructor's Manual" suggested as its first general question: "Draw up a list of ten heroes in American history." Making due allowance for the cult in such cult heroes I decided to go one better. I asked the class—strangers all—to draw up two lists, one of American heroes and one of heroes for all time, worldwide. They didn't have to sign their lists. We could take heroism from there, and write about it.

Collation of the lists submitted revealed the following ranking for American heroes: 1) Eldridge Cleaver, 2) Malcolm X, 3) Martin Luther King. Lincoln scored once, I think, but I don't recall seeing Washington's name at all. High scorers included Huey Newton (this was before the Newton-Cleaver feud), Bobby Seale, and a host of names obscure to me who turned out to have killed policemen or, better yet, a judge, for example, William Arthur Christmas, who removed a judge from a California courtroom and shot him to death. I cannot think why the New York City Fathers have not yet renamed Christmas Day after this new cult hero of our time.

Subventioned subversion seems to me the death-wish at its ripest. Guest lecturers are brought to our campus on the principle of affection for enemies, or anyone who hates America enough. A film on the Algerian revolution, showing French policemen shot in the back and innocent shoppers killed, is shown again and again, only surpassed in recurrence in some campus program, perhaps, by Truffaut's *400 Blows;* here we have a schoolboy stood in a corner for inattention, where he writes insulting graffiti about his master to whom he later lies and, as a result, has his face slapped by his father; this mistreatment (virtual mollycoddling compared to what we got in England in my youth) turns him into a typewriter thief, with whom, of course, we are supposed to sympathize. He has become a criminal and by a vulgarization of Freud, whereby crime is a liberation from a neurotic normality, the criminal has become our hero.

In the city colleges he has become institutionalized as such. After all, CCNY's penultimate President Buell Gallagher ordained a Malcolm X Day for the college. A scholarship fund has now been set up at CCNY in memory of a young instructress who spearheaded seizure of its South Campus during the 1969 riots, and whose chief attachment to the college seemed to be to want to tear it down; a new scholarship is now under way to commemorate a similarly minded ultra-revolutionary of those days, an Economics Professor who, described by Louis Heller as "the leader of the faculty group supporting the militants," changed his Jewish name to Conrad and finally shot himself in a field in Vermont.

It is, indeed, a stern lesson in radical chic to watch, over a period of years, the liberals' choice for election to this particular pantheon. Leary, in common with Charles Manson, lacked the right skin color. But Stokely Carmichael, Angela Davis, Rap Brown, Eldridge Cleaver had it (though Rap Brown employed two White lawyers when up for some crime or other). Professor Bruce Franklin, the pro-Maoist leader of Venceremos, and Robert S. Collier, Minister of Education for the New York Area Black Panthers, who tried to blow up the Statue of Liberty, also figured for a while, but the political record has been weird: Kwame Nkrumah, who was kicked out by his countrymen after wrecking the nation's economy, still seems to survive, as does Patrice Lumumba, though not Mobutu (brutal massacres of Black Africans by Black Africans, like those of the Hutu tribe by the Watusi, are conveniently ignored). Tom Mboya was admired as an agitator but when he became Kenya's economics minister, and supported a "cosmopolitan atmosphere" in Africa, he was met with rotten eggs in Harlem.

My present Chairman, Edward Quinn, a fighting radical with a grizzled beard, has written more recently in *Change* magazine of our students, "Little wonder that their hero is Walt Frazier of the Knicks or that they are attracted to a literary figure like Meursault in Camus' *The Stranger*." This purports to be an *in* statement (see how I keep up with basketball); in fact, in my experience "they" have never heard of Meursault and, when I have taken up Camus's masterpiece in class, their only interest in the principal character is his moral obliquity at the beginning and his killing of an innocent Arab. Of "the guns at Cornell," our President at the time, Buell Gallagher, wrote, "The whole nation sucked its breath shrilly when Black students with guns stood straight and proud before the photographers that day at Cornell. *That* was something!" When White students were arrested at Cornell at this time, their lawyers argued that it was racist to refuse to prosecute the Black militants beside them. Similarly, it was hard to know how to avoid being damned if you do and damned if you don't on our campus, when the president wanted to get a group of Black pushers of hard drugs removed; he summoned the police who, to avoid friction, sent Black officers to make the arrests. A student newspaper promptly stigmatized this action as biased—the sending in of Black police meant that they knew the offenders would be Black. Heads you win, tails I lose.

To return to my heroes, my surprise came in the second list I sent my students. This was again won handily by Cleaver (the name is an excellent one for an activist, anyway) with runners-up including Hitler, Mussolini, Lenin, Julius Caesar, Stalin, and good old Stokely Carmichael. It was a surprise since neither our text nor our media, nor even Kingman Brewster of Yale, had proposed the names of these dictators to the earnestly bowed heads before me. I became more surprised as I began to conduct conferences with Waynett and Greg and Julio, as with Opal and Marvina and Roseanne. Hitler had worked for his beliefs, I learned. He had been successful—for his *people*. Mussolini likewise.

Well, not quite, I objected gently. Both had brought their countries, masses of people, to destruction. One had killed himself in a kind of cellar, the other had been strung up by the heels from a lamppost in a side street—er, also by the people. "So what?" came the answer. "They all ganged up against him."

"Other *people*," I suggested, trying to touch that liberal lapel badge again.

"Hitler overran Europe and all but conquered Russia."

"I thought you liked Russia?" I was stung to reply. "Angela Davis does."

"What have you got against Hitler?" came the belligerent response to that.

"Plenty. He exterminated a rather large number of Jews."

"So what?"

It was hard to know what to say. A Black group with the jaw-cracking acronym COBATAME was shouting, from a full-page ad in the *New York Times* that day, for an end to the "racist policies of the state of Israel," as well as to the state itself. One of our student newspapers was urging the same, as was a majority of the UN, while a Queens College student paper had just been finally suspended for repeated anti-Semitism. Julius Lester rationalized this as follows:

> I think that it's a mistake, and a major mistake, to equate black antisemitism with the antisemitism which exists in Germany, in Eastern Europe, and in the Middle East. If black people had the capability of organizing and carrying out a program against the Jews, then there would be quite a bit of fear. (*Manhattan Tribune,* 2/15/69)

Odd reasoning, indeed. The good Blacks cannot be guilty of bad anti-Semitism, as the bad Arabs are; how come, then, the bad Arabs are also good Blacks? At least, they are when the need arises.

So our fugitive from justice becomes prime hero, or heroine. Angela Davis had made the FBI's "Ten Most Wanted" list, had she not, to say nothing of the cover of *Newsweek*? I scratched my head and searched my memory. For those of us who, in our uniformed youth, spent years fighting fascism, it was an odd feeling to be enlisted by the New York City school system as a sort of amanuensis to subversion. For the teaching of writing is largely the transmission of a message on paper; the mentor should presumably remain sweetly reasonable as regards content, impartial and apart.

"Look, Thelma," I would find myself telling some charming child whose only visible sign of imminent anarchy was an Afro so wide she had difficulty navigating my office door, "see, you've used *imperialist* four times in this paragraph, *racist* five, and *repressive* twice. Let's try something else here, just to sharpen your point, I mean."

"Chauvinist?" she supplied, suspiciously.

"Well, you've used that twice already, too."

"Paranoid?"

"Um."

"Colonialist?" Then decisively, with a sudden take-it-or-you're-racist *moue*—"Genocidal!"

Useless to tell Thelma that to say a word means something implies that it means that same thing more than once. She had used *imperialist* to convey as many messages as separate, almost indecipherable scrawlings in her two-page essay. Why worry? Her hero Cleaver had done the same.

One cannot blame them. They are simply following what society has now told them is the most easily accredited avenue to success. At New College, Oxford, it was Winchester. This time round to be Black and poor is the privileged position. Yet in realizing this, one cannot help noting an anomaly. Under the former system you could, if you failed, at least blame your failure on class prejudice. In the latter dispensation egalitarianism lays the burden of such failure squarely on your own shoulders. Unpalatable as it may be to have to admit it, race is today being used as a scapegoat for such failures in America. If you flunk your test it must be due to skin color—and your teacher is a racist. Anyone in American civic colleges is familiar with this escape route from reality by now.

So I see their point about Hitler, and indeed about Julius Caesar. Our social masochism is such that it deserves to be as shamelessly exploited as it is. John Fitzgerald Kennedy (removing the bubble from his car) showed to many a strong subconscious urge to suicide. The social anomie that

Kennedy induced in the nation—with every program he so beamingly began now flat on its face—came finally home to roost on the campuses of America. The generative principle behind the class I have described was that of Catherine of Russia to Diderot, "Your ideas are written on paper, ours have to be written on men's skins." I am convinced that if I had read out that ringing declamation to my open admissions class, Cathy would have scored high on our lists.

Perhaps it will be said that these helpless "ghetto kids" took their line from the media, where the criminal is indeed canonized. ("Squeaky" Fromme on the covers of both *Time* and *Newsweek* days after she had pointed a gun at President Ford.) Robbing a bank one day, on Cavett and Frost the next. You have but to write a book shocking or disaffiliated enough, and it is likely to be published. The liaison between rock culture and political radicalism is too well known to need reiterating here, a heady power combo in which you rush around the country singing about "street-fightin'" (like the Rolling Stones) to fabulous fees. There was money in those student riots. Abbie Hoffman's *Revolution for the Hell of It* was sold to MGM, Jerry Rubin's *Do It* being advertised, by Simon and Schuster, as "a Molotov cocktail in your very hands," while Random House put a cover on *Woodstock Nation* that showed their own building being bombed. Liberation gets incorporated into the name of a vaginal douche (The Liberation Spray) at the same time that we are cajoled into a movie about a huge youth-gathering in which an actual murder takes place, while Mick Jagger screeches away and, off at the side, promoters gossip about the likely cash receipts at the box office.

But there is more to the matter than what the media do; the dominant concept of the multiversity is what is truly factitious or (as Hutchins suggests) frankly inoperable, the heresy that "college is a microcosm of the world." It is not, nor should it be so. "The ideal of the American university," writes Buell Gallagher, who was President of ours, "includes within it the ideal of American society." It may do so, but it cannot be a democracy analogous to that of the outside world. In any event, Gallagher's statement occurs in the course of a rhapsody on Thomas Jefferson, who was the author of the American Declaration of Independence as well as the owner of over one-hundred-and-forty slaves.

The large urban university in America, like its new British "red-brick" counterpart, is a center to which students come for instruction and which they leave at the end of the day. It is the antithesis of that picture of Oxford sketched above, where you enjoyed the confidence and security of a communal social life first and foremost, and generally went for a good deal of instruction elsewhere. There were no campus pigs and student stealing was unknown.

Our municipal student has to support herself or himself by jobs in the workaday world. And the workaday world of the average American urban center includes some form of crime against the person for every one in three. The pretty eighteen-year-old brunette who reads pre-Raphaelite poetry with me in the morning comes up to the building through crime-ridden streets, teeming with junkies and other sick citizens, and she rides a subway back to her sweat-shop job thriving with lechers. It can be said that she never knew what it was to be young.

By this time the evidence is in about the state of the big city high schools. From Evan Hunter's *Blackboard Jungle* and Joan Dunne's *Retreat From Learning* to today's sagas of daily knifings, the record of the New York City high school is one of wholesale anarchy. It would be pitiable, if not so misguided. By an irony of history, the state of Eton under Keate at the start of the last century was just such a child ghetto, with the pupils jeering at the few masters, loosing rats on them during prayers, and the like. Our horror stories are by now routine. A Black CCNY coed writes:

> When I got to my class a white girl started hitting me and calling me names. I didn't say anything. I just looked at my teacher sitting there smiling. After two minutes of her hitting me I started telling her to leave me alone. This did it. All the white kids started calling me "chicken." I tried to hold my temper because I knew I could hurt her severely. After ten minutes of aggravation, the girl slapped me and said, "Beg, Nigger." I don't know what I did to her. All I know is, when my friends pulled me off, she was unconscious and blood was pouring from her nose. After being in shock for a couple of minutes I heard the voice of my teacher yelling. She was saying I was like Malcolm X and she would see that we Niggers never got ahead. I started punching her. I didn't hurt her, but I was satisfied just to be able to hit her.

This is scarcely an educational situation. Yet it is what happens daily in high schools in American cities. Here the criminal, the breaker of laws, is immediately authenticated as the dissident, which deprives true dissidents of any meaning; Rosa Luxemburg was far braver, in her lifetime, than Angela Davis has ever been so far, in hers. Reciprocally, China and Russia treat true dissidents as criminals, and rapidly eradicate both. New York City simply pays out $5 million a year repairing smashed school windows, and goes broke as a consequence.

I went to Oxford because my parents believed the place had some of the most competent teachers they could afford. It is a legend that Oxbridge fees of this era were very high; they were not; nor is Oxford today anywhere near first in UCCA selections made by British boys and girls; Sussex is. I did not like all my teachers, and I did not want to grow up to be like any of them, but I acknowledged that they had the authority of superior widsom. I was ignorant by comparison. But since authority is always seen as tyrannous by the American urban liberal, and destruction as justice, the stereotypical scene cited above is going to repeat itself and we shall continue to have the wasteful and repellent sight of cops in the classroom. This solves nothing.

Here the teacher is always wrong. Is there not something suspect in knowing more than someone else, in a public educational institution in America? The *New York Times* tells us, with a straight face, of a professor who felt so guilty of this aberration that he met his class sitting under the table, so that all were of equal rank. In one of my present classrooms I have repeatedly to push back chairs that the previous professor has arranged in a buddy-buddy ring. Professor Irwin Stark, who teaches Creative Writing at CCNY (as if all writing were not creative), tells us that "the more challenging alternative is for us to become students again." Why not? It is so much easier to celebrate incompetence and abrogate the responsibility of authority than make the effort to impart some form of discipline and structure to a young person's mind.

I take regular attendance on the basis that if there is a seat in the classroom unfilled, there is another under-privileged, disadvantaged worthy dying to occupy it. But I am one of the few who do take it; we are considered fascists as a result. A year ago the man who runs our Summer School told me of a student who had attended precisely two periods of an entire course and had come to him, in the new term, for help. This was a pleasant lad, who confessed that he had had to drop out due to family difficulties, and merely wanted a short-cut through our bureaucracy to discovering what grade he had been allotted, F or Inc (Incomplete) or whatever. He had been given a B.

Here is a New York high school teacher, Jerome McGovern, starting a class by handing out schedule sheets:

"You can see that this a schedule of the things we'll be reading this semester. I think you'll find these pieces. . . ." I didn't get "of literature" out of my mouth before guffaws swept the room. They all wanted to find a piece and other little puns. . . . "Please sit down. . . . Hey! Where are you going? Sit down. . . . Today I thought we might look at James Baldwin's . . ."

You are lucky, in some New York high schools, to have half the class left behind by the time you have finished roll call.

This is perhaps one thing. It is surely another to require a professor of higher education, such as the present author, to spend six years of his life getting a Ph.D. and then pay him over thirty thousand dollars of the taxpayers' money a year in order to pick up the darts made out of his course schedules, wake up the sleeping beauties in the back row, close the covers of comic books that other residents are reading, refer the openly bellicose to guidance counselors, and finally collect the blue books on which have been scrawled, under the space for the teacher's name (which name had been written on the board), Professor Whitey or Professor Kraut.

For the majority of my teaching life in America I have been lucky enough to be employed to do what I was trained to do, with such competence as I might summon to the task; but in a matter of a few years the people who now run the City University of New York have made my task one that could be performed by a janitor, albeit an expensive super and one more ready to receive abuse than most these days.

If you say that college *is* your society, and your society outside is a running chaos, then college will be the same. At meeting after meeting we mere teachers are reminded by our administrators of our responsibility to "the community." Where we are there is, in fact, no community; that of Hunter College would presumably include the Unilever Building, the Seventh Regiment Armory, and the Racquet and Tennis Club. Living within a longish stone's throw from our college, I can be said to live within the community, and I have noticed that it is a feature of those who shout most loudly about community indebtedness to live in Teaneck or Tenafly. Our Dean most vocal on the subject lives lavishly at the other end of Long Island, our present President in such a luxuriously appointed Madison Avenue duplex, with liveried servants, that a State audit alleging misuse of funds for his furnishings and rentals was thought serious enough to be featured prominently in the *New York Times*. Once more, it is all these breast-beating liberals who decide what our "community" is and who our "heroes" shall be. The Constitution, remember, was written by slave-owners, as was the work of that fascist hyena Sophocles, not to mention, more recently, Turgenev and Tolstoy.

The observance of a Malcolm X Day is decreed by liberal administrators against whose kind Malcolm himself railed incessantly, before he was wiped out by even more extremist Blacks. It is doubtful that either Gallagher or Marshak ever read a word of what Malcolm X wrote. His writings are an anthology of insults. Even Fanon is less fatuous. Yet, sure enough, a professor came solemnly forward, in the pages of *Columbia University Forum*, with a learned article on Malcolm's "rhetoric" (that is, abuse). Blacks like June Jordan and Toni Cade (styling herself, more recently, Bambara) spent much of their careers at our college insulting White teachers and, on graduation, were hastily invited back into the faculty. This version of academic America seems distinctly intent on destroying itself.

To institute an Afro Day, and import Ashanti tribesmen for it, would have seemed sheer Evelyn Waugh ten years ago. But to pay official homage to "Soledad Brother" George Jackson, killed while escaping from San Quentin in 1971, is a little lunacy. Both he and Angela Davis (Abelard and Heloise of the New Left, as they have been called) appealed seriously to the *New York Times'* Tom Wicker, who called Jackson "a potential leader and political thinker of great persuasiveness." Now a tape has been revealed on which Jackson confessed to the murder of a guard and wanted to take credit for "the events at Marin," where not only a judge but Jackson's own brother were killed. The Attica "heroes," in actual fact a minority among the prisoners, were equal dupes of the New Left, who persuaded them, as well as men like Jackson and Cinque, that America was fascist and thus encouraged the useless paranoia of their deaths. Jackson died quoting Ho Chi Minh.

These are the heroes of liberal academe. How curious that no administrator at our college ever enshrined a Jewish hero or heroine in this manner. There is no Ethel and Julius Rosenberg Day. Catholic France is more charitable, naming streets after Jewish resistance heroes and heroines, and victims of concentration camps. How remarkably patient our Jewish students have been in watching the heroic picked for them out of the frankly criminal. Will Hitler indeed be next? Idi Amin is much admired in Black student circles.

I cannot think of any country that is organizing so much hatred of itself in its educational system. Can you imagine a Russian Dean requiring his students to read and report on, say, William Buckley? And probably not even Russian universities are sending their young into the world thinking America to be Leary's "total lethal evil." Our ACLU, in a statement on higher education, is "committed to the protection of all peaceful nonobstructive forms of protest, including mass demonstrations, picketing, rallies and other dramatic forms"—as if any of our campus demonstrations were "peaceful." Our churches hurry to offer the "nonobstructive" SDS room for meetings if and when a college such as the University of Texas is benighted enough not to allow them on campus. The nearest case of loving one's enemies like this might be Marxist England of the thirties, but this was more a mood than official educational policy, and by now we know what tragedy it resulted in, to say nothing of the reams of recantations with which we have been deluged.

It seems that the liberal ethos has now been fully assimilated into the mainstream of American society, streaming from its cities. If you don't believe in equal rights, including the right to annihilate everyone who disagrees with you and to wreck America into the bargain, go elsewhere. Yet, despite this, injustices and inequalities still abound. So there is this accusation, like a suppurating wound, that the liberal ethos does not seem to have solved the ills of society, that, in fact, our society is growing ever more anarchic. Dogged hope is kept up that some day it will do so. In the meantime you try to institutionalize away the criminal ("he's sick") and ignore the persistent and steady erosion of the quality of life.

Every so often the *New York Times* will come out with an editorial on the dreadful tyranny of corporal punishment in the schools. It did so recently after it had sent a reporter into a Black-ghetto high school that had been rescued from total anarchy by a Black principal and two Black aides who were so inclement as mildly to employ a paddle on the backsides of delinquents; the caning that goes on in England and Sweden and Switzerland, the democracies with a high respect for private property, would probably have quite unhinged this reporter.

But the concern of the *Times* here backfired when a majority of Black parents came out behind the Principal, endorsed his corrective activities, and told Whitey to mind his own business. If you refuse to recognize the existence of aggression, and try to syphon it off as so much psychological disturbance, you will get what you have in New York today, a homicide rate that horrifies the world, barring Detroit, whose goes higher. Nearly everyone at our college has some mugging story in or around it by now. My wife, who teaches in our Art Department, was thrown down some stairs for denying entry to a gang of Black youths who wanted to see "pussy" (a nude model in her class), while a colleague was raped in the Ladies' Room. City College had four rapes plus one victim sodomized on its campus in the spring term of 1975, while in the *first month* of the winter 1975 semester at Hunter there were three rapes in its halls. It's bad all over, as they say.

Let one final instance suffice: where we live, the subway surfaces and mounts high over the street to the nearest station. Three stalwart iron staircases lead up to it. Until recently there was an up escalator to the platform, but local youths, all doubtless unpaddled, so persisted in riding on the runners at the side and thus stalling the machine that the city finally refused to go on repairing the moving staircase. The aged and toddlers and heart-weak must now climb up the stairs. Every slot machine I have tried in Harlem—and I have lived there for many years—is today slugged beyond repair. It is the same with the public telephone. Meanwhile, the subway systems of Paris (with its unviolated first-class seats), Munich, and London rumble on their ways unvandalized.

In such cities, in Japan, Sweden, Switzerland, and to a lesser extent England, there is an agreement about something called society. In urban America it is disagreement that is honored first. For since, despite the liberal ethos, society is still so far from ideal, any critic must be protesting social injustice. The disruption of a classroom, and its denial to other participants, is no more reprehensible than a peace march that stops city traffic and delays an ambulance from getting an emergency case to the hospital.

Since society is at many points corrupt, anyone who acts against it is liable to become a potential hero. Surely civil disobedience was what Martin Luther King was involved in. His widow was honored at our last commencement. The criminal and reformer are in partnership. Our college bookstore sold FREE ANGELA and FREE CLIFFORD buttons side by side. This marked more than the triviality of much dissent; it said that, since Angela Davis and Clifford Irving were both in prison, they were both critics of society, equipollent in appeal. In this embrace almost any common criminal, provided his crime is spectacular enough, may acquire the halo of reformer.* Women's year was celebrated by the exempla of "Squeaky" Fromme, Emily Harris and Indira Gandhi.

It was Professor Douglas Stewart of Brandeis who proposed that, since so many student heroes have been jailbirds (Socrates, Cicero, St. Paul, Dante, Galileo, Paine, Marx), there should be a program established called The Junior Year in Jail: "A student who is placed in a city or county jail will receive a pass degree. Those who are sentenced to state prisons will be granted the degree of cum laude. Those who reach federal penitentiaries will be graduated magna cum laude." He concluded:

If existing prisons are found to be inadequate to receive all such students, the foundations could probably be approached by the university for matching funds to construct last-resort jails on university campuses for underprivileged students who do not have the training to get into regular jails.

---

*In 1976 New York's Community School Board 5 replaced Mayor La Guardia's name for a public school with that of Pedro Campos, a would-be assassin of President Truman.

5
The Collapse of the Curriculum

Evidence of the manner in which the humanities seem ever intent on destroying themselves comes annually from their built-in Trojan horse, the MLA or Modern Language Association. Each year this body meets at various points of the Union and is a barometer of academic fads, with a flesh market on the side where perspiring aspirants strive to get employed. I must have been attending these gatherings, on and off, for more than a quarter of a century by now. In the fifties they were strictly suit-and-tie affairs; the odd tweedy or corduroyed English don about looked untidy. A few years ago the milling throngs resembled so many extras hanging around some Old Testament epic organized by De Mille. The combination was described by Anthony Burgess as a mixture "of frontiersman and guru." At the 1971 meeting our President told us that the teaching of literature was no longer a valid objective in higher education; at the end of 1973 an MLA committee issued a report on academic freedom, published in its journal.

Now academic freedom, like pregnancy, is an absolute. It either exists or does not exist. But here was the leading professional body of the humanities in this country redefining this right from an AAUP (American Association of University

Professors) statement of 1940, to which it had subscribed, to suit the new and swinging times: "Academic freedom is not an elitist concept. It is the exercise, in academic settings, of the freedom that all Americans have, under the First Amendment to the Constitution, to speak and write." It did not take CUNY Physics Professor Miro Todorovich long to observe that this statement would be an occasion for hilarity, were it not so deadly serious. Deadly, in truth, for the factional rewriting of an abiding principle evinces yet again the death wish of academe. You commit suicide by denying to teaching the status of a profession, and then put on sackcloth and ashes when no students show up.

For of course academic freedom is an earned right and, as such, can be called elitist in the same sense that you might call my doctor's right to set my limbs elitist, or my lawyer's or dentist's or accountant's to administer to my needs and charge me fees. By assigning the precious dignity of academic freedom to the role of an inalienable civil right, granted by the Bill of Rights to member citizens of a democracy, the MLA is saying that anyone has the right to teach, so long as he has a voice.

The First Amendment was designed to protect all, not special classes of individuals. But, as Todorovich points out, "because a person who wishes to be a physician has a right as a citizen to speak and write, this does not mean he has a right to practice medicine." To say that academic freedom is something "that all Americans have" is to depose teaching from the rank of a profession and to imply that it is open to everyone. Anyone can teach, and anyone does. If you are as determined to sabotage yourself as this, why bother to pick up your monthly paycheck?

"Ideally," concedes the report, in an obvious sop to those it considers reactionaries, "we might define academic freedom, from the point of view of scholars and teachers in the language disciplines, as the right to compose, speak, write, print, record or circulate any combination of sounds or letters whatsoever." Todorovich footnotes this statement as follows: "'Ideally,' in other words, an idiot or anyone who mouths any combination of sounds or writes any combination of letters (gibberish) has a right to academic freedom, has a right to teach as part of his birthright as a citizen in a Bill of Rights democracy." What, then, of mathematics? Frankly, I could say that there have been moments in my career at City College when a knowledge of karate might have been the most pertinent professional qualification.

Behind this capitulation of standards the Medusa head of social action rises slowly to turn the terrified professoriat into stone. Once again, you may learn by experience, but experience doesn't guarantee learning. MLA promises to consider "problems such as that of relevance in the classroom, and how far literature is a value in itself and how far it is a weapon to be used in the battle of social change." This is, as the French say, exact. The chief professional organization of the humanities in America regards ideas as weapons, literature as what it does, not what it is. Here is the most virulent kind of skepticism. Eldridge Cleaver is worthless as literature—but he seemed for a while, notably when serving a sentence for rape rather than trying to lecture at Berkeley, to muster some attention to his so-called ideas. Proust did not. However, there are those who dare feel that Proust's ideas are closer to the truth.

So academic freedom is naturally elitist and the professoriat, like the legal or medical body, an elite. However, this makes the liberal intellectual feel guilty, and he has to keep on whittling down the stilts on which his house of intellect is built. My butcher has the right to free speech (and frequently uses it) but not, yet, to academic freedom. Nor has my latest foul-mouthed, back-seat guerrilla, flaunting the colors of the Hohenzollern Empire on his beret, lounging on his ear and occasionally expectorating his contempt of Pope. In the major city colleges we have been schooled to endure daily obscenity and insolence under this public misapprehension. But, if our professional body disallows academic freedom the status of earned right, we can be quite sure that no one in authority is going to lend a hand when finally we take a swing at the punk.

As regards literature as "a value in itself," it is enlightening to listen to Frederick Olafson speaking on the philosophy of the curriculum at Rockefeller University in 1974: "My guiding assumption here is that the character of the curriculum in any given field is a function of the presiding conception of the objectives and methods of scholarship within that field." This virtually disqualifies the humanities as taught in our large urban colleges, since in them the humanistic curriculum has been turned into so much civil service. Here we are involved in social repair first and foremost, and any independence of immediate purpose must be suspect. We must plunge into the vortex of social "action." To offer a *detached* imaginative study to the U. S. Government for support from such a center would be supererogatory. Yet such detachment has been the glory of the humanities which, both Western and Chinese, ask us among other things to stand aside and be interested in ourselves as persons, not as so many castes and group-rhythms.

More than history or philosophy, art and literature are committed to imaginative man. They deal with imaginative works men have created, have written or painted or sculpted. Handling the mythical and irrational, these works have been of immense value to man's psyche over a long period. But this use cannot be "proved" and the imaginative act often seems, at first glance, to violate empiricism. It is not congenial to science, at least not to the science of the American city.

Hence, when the attack on the arts curriculum became full-blooded at the end of the sixties, one feature of sidelining the humanities for the aggrandizement of the sciences was an attack on any abiding principle in the arts. They were denigrated as mere matters of subjective preference. You like James Jones; I prefer Andrew Marvell.

American society was in flux, as exemplified on campus by the rote of unopposed riots, so that few cognitive standards could be derived from contemporary man by which to refer the humanistic inquiry to a student's life in any big city. You studied passing interests. You felt vaguely guilty at finding Spenser and Milton, both apparently paragons of the language you were trying to use, over your head and so you took it out on the world outside. The result is now apparent when you compare the literary curricula of New York City colleges with those of some large state institution of, say, the rural West. You might be reading another literature altogether, and usually are. A momentum of study is going on in both places, but the degree of ambiguity that has crept in is such as to make for a very great loss of belief in literature, indeed for widespread skepticism. It must be said that this skepticism in the humanities *owes* to the fact that the contemporary American classroom has to sideline a lot of what is spiritual (rather than wholly intellectual), thanks to the variety of religious opinions. The Song of Solomon simply isn't a vegetation rite for the pious Jews in my classes.

It is true that graduate schools still require some evidential study in the humanities. Sometimes the *Forschung* method of our graduate humanities and, in particular, the habit or tic of interior analysis of literature, seem liabilities more than assets, attempts by those losing ground to shore up their ruins and stand up tall to the sciences. But literature is written in language which, in a phrase, is too close to itself (and therefore "sucks"); its manifestations are too metaphoric and illusory for a sedulously scientific civilization. So the first conceptual ordering of our literary curricula to go was the historical. We scrapped survey courses of English literature years ago, generally substituting genre courses, and we are now in the absurd situation of considering reinstating those surveys simply in order to have the feeling we are teaching something, in order to have available some common body of knowledge with which to sent out a graduate.

The only way that the group of us working to restore historical surveys to our literary curriculum could attract votes for the proposal was to present it as a change, for our curriculum is today under constant manic alteration. Indeed, one noted anthropologist, George Pettitt, has called America's faith in change "an acquired abnormality." Americans, he tells us, look forward to change much as Muslims hope to enter heaven on a white horse. "Modern American civilization might well be characterized as a culture dedicated not only to the indefinite promotion of change but to the infinite expansion of specialties." So writes Pettitt in a classic statement that could be put over the gravestone of the college curriculum in the humanities today. To invent the new every semester, as in proposing some new course, is to evade evaluation, since the new is not, in this case, amenable to any norms of judgment.

Much has by now been written about the Great-Books-burger sponsored by Robert M. Hutchins, as President of Chicago, as a first attenuation of the arts curriculum. The Wisconsin Integrated Liberal Studies Program was something of the same. But at least you read something when you followed a Great Books course. Today Hutchins would surely see many of our genre courses as extremely destructive of mind, and he has in fact confessed that "the multiversity does not appear to be a viable institution" (October 1967).

However, as the student was hurried on from one literary peak to another, no teacher could hope to enter in depth into the periods assigned; the man expert in fifth-century BC Athenian civilization could not be expected to deal as well with eighteenth-century German literature and nineteenth-century Russian and Norwegian works—particularly not in a college as polyglot as our own where original speakers of these languages are likely to abound in any given class. So since you could not enter into any depth, you relied on width; you associated your imperious Great Books, your Dante and Milton, with immediate concerns in the student's background, rather than with those of the originating epochs.

There were several effects of this divorce, the alimony of which we are only truly paying today. The Great Books program at least had the virtue of being, as a rule, chronological. It had a sense of direction rather than mere movement. For man is chronological. All too often the contemporary student reads an author because the present class simply followed upon the last in the manner of the schoolboys at the end of *Buddenbrooks*, who confess, "we don't say, for instance, that it is nearly half-past twelve. No, we say, 'It's nearly time for the geography period.!'"

Our understanding of the past and our records of human experience are vital to our survival. Animal species have not improved their knowledge over the centuries, as has man. It is true that animals possess instinctual awarenesses far superior to those of humans (notably the olfactory), but the beast has no means of transmitting learned information from generation to generation. Alfred Korzybski called this peculiarly human faculty "time-binding." A deer cannot tell another deer that their common grandfather was killed by a cougar when sheltering under the same ledge where they are now. No ape can tell another ape *why* he dislikes or is afraid of him. Human language, on the other hand, stores a past and conveys causality from it. To paraphrase the philosopher Santayana, If you don't learn from history you're condemned to repeat it.

Historicity is an index of human consciousness. It has seldom been under such attack in humanistic study as now. There seems some real bias against historical knowledge in our liberal arts, while, over in Einstein Hall, the waves of pop culture make no impression on Math. Sequential study implies a certain hierarchy of knowledge and can only parenthetically concern itself with the passing tastes and interests of sundry individuals aged from seventeen to twenty-two. Hence the old Introduction to Literature courses were scrapped and a variety of genre courses (Poetry, Drama, Fiction) substituted for them. When in his moving auto-biography Leonard Kriegel tells of trying to teach in the Dotheboys' Hall of New York's City College, he claims that the old survey course "certainly worked better than the amorphous courses that have since been substituted for it, in which students choose between genre courses and such plums as 'Varieties of Heroism'. . . .The survey course was far less paternalistic than what was to be substituted for it." Kriegel, a polio victim who uses crutches, has recounted how difficult it is physically to get to class these days, so overcrowded has City College become.

As I write, what have generally been substituted are called in our case Core courses, those, it is (still paternal-istically?) assumed, which form the *core* of a humane education; there are no historical surveys of literature left at all, although some faculty now want to restore them. In the place of a survey you study a genre. It is not the same. Once more you sacrifice a great deal of what literature means for instant intensity. In Drama and Fiction it is likely that teachers will select as many foreign works as English, in a department of the latter name.

Why not? For one thing you are going to read Shakespeare against works that have been filtered through and usually damaged by translation. Obviously students should have access to Zola and Ibsen and Tolstoy, all of whom translate well; but Goethe loses out when he has to be retranslated (until recently) from the Victorian elegist Bayard Taylor made of him. It is all very well to abandon a historical survey for an "exciting," hepped-up group of plays or stories from five literatures, all of them post-1830, but you end up, as teacher, neither Ben Jonson's guide nor instructor; you are simply another fellow reader laying a mind alongside theirs as you breeze through Lorca and Ionesco and Brecht.

The next step in the movement to disburden the student of the tyranny of the required curriculum was, as with us, to relieve him of any requirements at all and then lure him into humanities courses by virtue of their social concerns. This has been a drastic form of surgery, one California State college listing such courses as *Relevant Recreation in the Ghetto* and *The Selection and Preparation of Soul Food*. Students are interested in the occult? Then institute a course on the Black Arts, and How to Work a Planchette or Ouija board. A year or so ago *Faust* began to take on a new magnetism in one of my courses; I realized that this was owing to Goethe's treatment, and mistreatment, of magic in the work. What of Chinese Studies? Macrobiotic Cooking?

SUNY's Old Westbury College (State University of New York) now grants a B.A. in Women's Studies. At first glance this seems socially logical and responsible; there are still not many women administrators in American colleges, women preponderating among elementary school teachers, junior librarians, and children's book editors. By now women's studies have been set up almost everywhere, the majority during the past five years. With the best will in the world one has to realize that somewhere along the line someone is going to ask just what worth these degrees have, what was the *content* of such courses. If you read *Jane Eyre* and *Madame Bovary* in your women's studies courses, well and good—even if you did so through a glass darkly. However, if what you did was to learn vaguely what it means to be a woman in New York in the nineteen seventies, so much common sense for most conscious women, then who is going to be impressed by a *summa cum laude* in Fem Lib?

Similarly, I began to get Mad Hatteritis when summoned to listen not long ago to our new leading light of a liberal arts Dean, charming, handsome, personable, who assembled a number of us to advocate, rhapsodically, the alterations he proposed in our outmoded and retrograde humanities curriculum. He proposed cross-cutting or "interdisciplinary" courses—discipline always being read by such minds as a restraining rather than enlarging element—in Alienation. Each department would have a core of courses on this subject since, he argued, our students were alienated. We stared at each other—*forty credits in Alienation to graduate*. A stirring contempt for former structures was the order of the day, but you can scarcely be competent in Alienation. After all, to be perpetually impermanent is hardly to exist. The idea was that, since we taught "ghetto kids," we should share their pressing problems and encourage them to affirm some mystical inner identity by a rabid diet of alienated authors—some of whom, judging by their bank balances, didn't seem alienated to me in the slightest. Each class would thus be an effortless reverie, with "Teach" a buddy, even less authoritarian than the analyst he was standing in for. This is far from a fantasy. It happened. The taxpayer paid for it.

Once more into the void, dear friends, once more—and close the wall up with high purposes. As the teachers stagger off into forty credits of Alienation they are investigating untested terrain. Will a degree in Alienation really support our students in later life? Will it help? Or will another softly smiling, even more highly paid Dean advance with another program, entirely dissimilar, perhaps even the reverse? The medieval guild also, in Jacques Barzun's words, "undertook to do everything for the town," but it didn't have over a quarter of a million students in it. The historical survey had certain proven qualities since we live historically and time is a unit of our being. We repeat. Our hearts beat, our human processes recur. In actual fact, the urban bureaucracy alienates all of us, not only "ghetto kids." Do we really want to unanchor our students in this manner, and lead them backwards into primitivity and terror, turning ourselves into so many aesthetic wolf-men? For here the artist's true possibilities, transmuting the animistic for us, become vital; we deride art by saying that it was all Alienation.

To oppose this degeneracy is to be met with frosty looks at faculty meetings and cold shoulders in corridors. For in truth the liberal humanist scarcely knows the true destruction he is effecting on art. As the sense of history slackens and loses hold, turns into "interps," we try to achieve some kind of spurious momentum by erasing past culture and, since we cannot quite be left with nothing, intensifying the status of heroes. Professor Olafson has observed: "it would be best to acknowledge that by comparison with the dramatic intensity of the world of myth or of the titanic self-assertion that produces its own myths, humanism is a non-starter."

As has been indicated above, this has been made particularly clear of late in Black Studies, where any White culture, even (perhaps especially) Jewish, is defined as that which is politically weak and effete, to be regarded as so much debris to sweep away. In place of this tolerant and plural bric-a-brac of the past anything obsessive is admirable—Rap Brown, Eldridge Cleaver, even the disastrous Kwame Nkrumah and Patrice Lumumba. Anthologies pour out on such "heroes." You are ordained to study those who have been in definite opposition, to revere antinomies, huge mythic figures. It helps if these are vague or dead, like Hitler or "General" Cinque. Nietzsche is strongly admired by most activist Blacks I have had in class. Figures like these have divorced themselves brutally from "bourgeois" humanist morality. Such courses, then, will occupy themselves little with the actual life of men as they are. From Attila to Attica, you might say.

Yet the most extreme of these programs seem to go on getting regularly savaged by those who take them. In May 1974 our Black student newspaper published a list of "theses to Black Study Departments collected from students." Thesis I concluded: "we need revolutionary instructors, not diplomats." Thesis II began, "Education is bourgeoise, and, at a white campus, it is also integrationist for Black students. Education for Blacks must incorporate the *state-of-the-art* knowledge and forfeit the integrationist trash." In Thesis V we were told: "After each semester of instruction, Black Studies' Professors, Associate Professors, Assistant Professors, and Lecturers should be put on trial by the students they taught." Thesis VII was the rip-off: "Who the hell needs Black Studies? Black people sure don't. A degree in Black Studies might as well be written on toilet paper for all the use and mileage one can attain out of it. . . ." For this, too, the taxpayer paid.

Humanistic knowledge helps answer the question, Who am I? It does so by relating man to his past and, by implication, to his probable future. The establishment of Black Studies programs is a perhaps inadvertent admission of this principle, seeking to define Negritude by locating it in a past. The latest "relevant" study, on the other hand, endeavors to confer a ready-made identity tailored to fit what the customer wants, a fashionable group identity instead of that of a meaningful individual; and in a few years' time the customer may want another identity altogether. By joining in this race, teachers get involved in impossible ambiguities of their mystery and usually just surrender by becoming buddies. The ethnic studies innovation may have been a politically praiseworthy aim, but it soon became clear that you couldn't go on, term after term, for fifteen weeks of classroom work each semester, studying who you were. Programs of this nature began to be abandoned where they were not opposed by other Blacks (e.g., Martin Kilson at Harvard). Ours were almost empty until content was injected, whereupon official-dom realized that expensive duplication was taking place, Music Two, let us say, finding itself taught in at least three different divisions of the university, to a handful of students (and with all sorts of specious excuses) in each.

The social sciences became equally afflicted, for in them there are no invariant properties, only "findings"; and findings depend on passing concerns, which can be and are replaced with another set very readily. Inventing your own curriculum as you go along can be singularly unoriginal; students, in Barzun's words, "propose changes which, if adopted, are invariably reversed by the next participants, all unaware that they are advocating the reactionary *status quo ante*." Nathan Glazer notes that at Harvard only Jewish Studies have elicited a lively student response to the ethnicity stakes and observes that in this case there is something to study:

It is my understanding that it is not only at Harvard that we have seen a surprising drop in enrollments in various introductory and general education courses in the social sciences, and an even more surprising loss of favor of certain newer efforts of the social sciences to respond to contemporary concerns, for example, Afro-American studies and urban studies. Jewish Studies seem to be flourishing, but because of their content—Hebrew texts, history— they are closer to the humanities than to the social sciences, which bears out my general point.

Glazer's general point is amply borne out in an article on Black Studies in *The American Scholar* (Autumn 1969) by John Blassingame of the University of Maryland. "When I ask Black students what are the goals of Afro-American studies, I often get a blank stare," Blassingame tells us. He tells us too of a Black student who, in a stormy committee meeting, demanded the creation of a Black Studies Department, but who, when asked what its objectives were to be, walked out of the room for answer. It would seem that in such instances you have the paradox of young people who are hopelessly vague about the purposes of a course of study, yet who have made up their own minds about it, in any case. Blassingame concludes:

> When the black students at a California college complained that they were being used as resource persons in a "Racism in America" course, a separate all-black section was established with a black psychologist as the teacher. The reaction of the students to the course was mixed. One group told me that it was a great course because the teacher required no reading; allegedly, since all the blacks understood white racism, they simply met and "rapped" with each other. The more astute students described the course as a "bull session" where everybody "got down on whitey."

Numerous Black as well as White scholars have insisted on Glazer's general point, which again devolves upon teaching a subject rather than a student. To have a bull session in which everyone gets down on Whitey may prove fortifying to the internal morale of a few students for a few minutes, but to institute this as a course of study for an entire semester helps no one, least of all Blacks. It perhaps helps presidents. Andrew Brimmer, a trustee of Howard University, says that Blacks "should have no illusions about the extent to which they are likely to acquire in 'Black Studies' programs the mental discipline, technical skills and rigorous training in problem-solving that they will so desperately need in their future careers." He adds, "Rarely does one see faculty members (in whose hands a college curriculum must rest) coming forth to tell Black students that some of their proposals and views are simply nonsense—as some of them certainly are." The passing craze for Swahili—Claudia Polly giving a daily lesson over WABC, and dashikis compulsory in the classroom—was certainly just such nonsense, unless you planned removing permanently to Mombasa or Zanzibar. In Anthony Burgess's words:

> Black Studies don't, in fact, exist, any more than do White Studies. A course that encloses St. Augustine, Toussaint L'Ouverture, Coleridge-Taylor, Paul Robeson and Papa Doc, because they are all black, is as absurd as one that deals with Robert Louis Stevenson, Joseph Stalin, Mark Twain and Salvador Dali because they all had moustaches.

So the students don't seen to be buying the new glib "relevance." They see that the sciences have remained unchallenged by cultural populism—they can't rewrite Physics One each term, as they can their humanities courses, in order to suit current enthusiasms. Since science alone stands unscathed in the curriculum, then, it achieves a rare dignity, and the irony obtains that the institution everywhere encouraging detestation of "the military-industrial complex" feeds its sons and daughters into that very system.

One last effort to be "interdisciplinary" seems, indeed, designed to try to meet this paradox. This is the insertion of "media" into the humanities courses, usually by those who do not know what a medium is. These offerings are presently running wild everywhere, with textbook publishers chasing after them sycophantically. For the most part, what they mean is seeing film or TV (often authenticated as "visual thinking," though the one point about Rudolf Arnheim's famous book of that name was that for human beings visual thinking isn't conceptual thinking). The rationale for these courses is again dithyrambic: since students are all watching TV, you should watch it with them, and so join in the dance.

Our own college catalogue now bristles with literature-and-media courses; there is even a seminar on avant-garde film ("from Pop to Conceptual, Films of Godard, Resnais, Warhol, Cocteau; art of Oldenberg, Lichtenstein, Warhol; Readings in Warhol, Robbe-Grillet, and Barthelme"). We hear of "audiotutorial trips," full of "tape scripts," "learning modules," and "peer interaction." Our Distinguished Professorships, for which the taxpayer coughs up close on forty thousand dollars a year each, have not gone to distinguished professors at all, but to novelists who have just had successful movies made of one of their fictions—Joseph Heller, Anthony Burgess, Kurt Vonnegut, in that order.

There is nothing very "interdisciplinary" about these courses. You do not breach the chaste exclusivities of any departmental system by showing films of fiction (as I have been made to do) or listening to the latest rock combo. You simply succeed once more in degrading high art. Irving Howe is explicit on the subject:

> Under no conditions, however, would I assent to proposals for removing serious texts from the already unsatisfactory genre courses and instead using "media" or "communications" or "relevant" materials. That is no longer a compromise, it is a craven surrender.

But the Irving Howes are in a minority among us. Through high school the American city child attends a series of classes from early September to late June. Generally, there are six of these classes a day, each averaging some forty minutes. "It is an involvement," writes Paul Lissandrello, "which requires the attention span and diligence of most jobs pursued by parents and he or she looks forward to the day's end as eagerly as a factory worker, lawyer, or technician." By the end of high school he or she has spent twenty thousand hours in front of the Boob Tube *at home alone.* At home he or she learns, Professor Lissandrello tells us, the "economics" of shopping, the "social dynamics" of dating, the "social psychology" of watching *All in the Family* on television. One has perhaps repeatedly to remind the reader of this book that this is no satire by Huxley or Waugh; it is actually happening, funded by public monies.

For the most part these classes, in New York City at any rate, will have taken place in ill-lit, roach-ridden, fire-hazard rooms with posters of Malcolm X and Che Guevara on the walls, and Eldridge Cleaver paperbacks curling and yellowing on radiators. Simply to stop the noise and get some sort of attention, teachers reach increasingly for the multimedia package that knowing publishers are preparing for them. The attention span sinks further still. The inner task of fantasy is thinned as everything gets enacted outside the child. A restless sensationalism seeps in and tries to fill out a vacuum without rules or restrictions or requirements. This is our real crime against children, polluting their minds with the ready-made fantasies of adults. Little wonder that New York has more deaths from heroin among teenagers than from all childhood diseases put together, while its homicide rate is over ten times that of London or Tokyo.

The product of this chaos is then invited into a free college. Helping hands are extended on all sides. Here he hopes to stand aside for a second, forget or try to sideline something of the "economics" of shopping for a time, and acquire some form of intellectual structure. It is the obligation of the teacher, placed on him by the adults of the community, to supply such; and in the sciences this still happens. But in the humanities our high school graduate finds an increasing number of anti-intellectuals all gleefully assassinating themselves by reaching for the cassette and the film instead of believing in their subject.

This is our treason of the clerks. It used to be that values were transmitted by example, but within less than a generation our liberal academic is teaching by misexample, trying more and more frantically to look like his students, wearing this year's serape, last year's love-beads, his hair and beard ever longer and filthier, his speech carefully peppered with the latest "in" *argot* and obscenity. No wonder the student cannot look up to these highbrow clowns. In fact, he comes to regard them with contempt, one expressed, we shall see, in the fury he feels at having to be evaluated by such buffoons.

For the easiest way out is to throw up your hands and say, The student knows best. Daniel Boorstin took care of the "relevance" fad once and for all when he wrote, "Education is learning what you didn't even know you didn't know." Meanwhile, school and higher boards sit back and smile at the confusion and self-destruction. Bring on the tape recorders and closed-circuit screens; it will be one teacher less to pay. Where I work, we have Deans with bafflingly abstract titles (Administration . . . Institution) whose jobs, apart from the parking of faculty cars and the subsequent collections of sizable paychecks, are to make classrooms into auditoria, more "productive" and more McLuhanly impersonal and deadly.

In all this the tragicomic element is that the liberal mind that has Pied Pipered Johnny into this miseducation seriously thinks it is performing a service. We have opened the doors, made open admissions work because we say they work, and we owe it to these kids to ready them for a role in life, as well, of course, as to arrive at a verdict of total success on ourselves. The operation is a Minificat to the Gross National Product. Lissandrello's representative terminology shows as much: to call dating "social dynamics" is not to make home an extension of school so much as to make school an extension of home. Everything is enjoyable, or should be. It is the hedonism of *Playboy*. As a teacher, one can only view the watching of *All in the Family* on TV as "social psychology" as the pouring of derision on social psychology and, of course, on yourself.

Under this aegis the curriculum has to collapse, since higher education is seen as an emergency service station into the going society, a supermarket in which you learn how not to write in multi-media "labs" or "rap rooms" and end up grading your own papers. By this token there is no reason why the "mechanics" of fixing your car may not rate as educative, as worthy of college credit as Shakespeare.

This liberal, then, is the least revolutionary or subversive person around. He is merely continuing, running into its grave, a movement initiated in England after the Education Act of a century ago. Keeping Johnny vertical by means of media is consenting to, not criticizing, the worst of TV. Anyone who stands aside from this whirlpool of philistinism is reactionary ("traditionalist"). At a recent curriculum conference I asked one Dean after his speech advocating more and more media what he expected literature Ph.D.'s to do about it all; he snapped back, "You've got to recycle yourselves." The machine metaphor tells its tale. We are meshing students into the standard society like cogs. The role of the thinker is dead. And literature is no longer a value. It is, rather, *pace* the MLA, "a weapon to be used in the battle of social change."

Irving Kristol has shown how this obligatory innovation in the curriculum has now seeped down from the colleges into the secondary systems, where it has become methodologically enshrined; for when all is said and done, the high schools take their examples from the colleges, and so down the line. Ronald Berman, Chairman of the National Endowment for the Humanities, revealed in a *New York Times Magazine* article some of the most bizarre projects imaginable put up to him for funding, from courses in which everyone taught everyone else to "the substitution of the comics for the classics, of the Beatles for Dr. Johnson." In short, don't teach your subject, teach your society—whatever that is.

This restless and evasive search for the solution to local concerns *now* wounds the arts particularly. Yet these we are, as humanities professors, employed to serve. Instead, we have become addicted to following trends. Take art itself. From abstract expressionism our museum directors and art teachers rushed admiringly to Pop Art, to Op Art, to environmental art, Art Brut, earthworks, photorealism, conceptual art. The Sculls are said to be trying to unload examples of them all.

Someone pulls in off the New Jersey Turnpike and picks up a load of *Dreck*. The Whitney Museum installs it on a floor. The unsuspecting pay money to come in to see what has been validated by the pundits. But the pundits refuse their role (the University of Washington's Free University, for instance, offered virtually any course given by anybody). The pundits decline to evaluate; they are simply illustrating society to itself, not exhibiting art; there is no jurisprudence left in the latter field at all. They throw up their hands and say, with Tom Hoving, We are simply showing what is going on. Faced with this abject cowardice and confronted by what passes for art today, Baudelaire would have shared the sentiments of the French peasant shown a camel for the first time—"I don't believe it."

Nor is it easy to shock any more, even in academe. After all, *Deep Throat* is down the street; the Damiano brothers are making more money than the whole of the CUNY professoriat put together. The celebrated St. Louis sex researchers, Dr. William Masters and Mrs. Virginia Johnson, got a grant from the U.S. Public Health Service, no less, to photograph and tabulate sexual intercourse, and are by now minor folk heroes.

An "artist" shows sculptured excrement in a New York gallery and the *New York Times* merely yawns—"These aggregations of colonic calligraphy contain many formal excellencies . . . ." Turd Art!

The same directionless but ceaseless motion, personified by those in the antechamber of Dante's hell, possesses our literature studies. Surveying old catalogues, I scratch my head: who reads the once adulated Kerouac any more? Or Christopher Fry? Who is Bernadine Dohrn? Dottie Palombo? Micki Leaner? The Beats, the Hips, the Yippies came and went. *Vengano e vanno.* But yet their writings were given to suffering students for examinations. To what purpose? Apparently, the substance of the humanities course must now be so much *Zeitgeist*; as with the craze for "media," you try to make over classroom work into something more current, and therefore more valid.

We no longer know what we value in art. This void is filled by constant change. Each term we add new courses and scrap others, terrified that we might become, for a moment, *retardataire.* At meeting after meeting I have heard professors told that it would be going backwards to reinstate survey courses in literature. But perhaps going backwards is going forwards for once. "Lyrical enthusiasm about defeat" is what Wyndham Lewis called this demon of progress in the arts.

By its agency we once again worship science. The critical anarchy of the liberal arts professor is another aspect of his lack of confidence in his own *métier.* Any tradition is automatically reactionary. When assigned an Imaginary Worlds genre course recently, I scheduled Homer, Plato, Lucian, More, Bacon, and was considered hopelessly dogmatic —except by the students. I should have listed Tolkien (who would have detested these trends) and Henlein and perhaps Asimov. We do not allow ourselves to reflect that the latest fad outmodes another, which was, in its day, cherished for originality.

For to worship the new is the easiest way of being relieved of aesthetic judgment. As Chairman of UCLA's Art Department Lester D. Longman put it, "Michelangelo's art was very original during his life time, but El Greco's would not be until nearly three hundred years after his death." (Equally, Gerard Manley Hopkins was highly "original" well after his death.) In one movie the Marx Brothers gallivanted around, playing absurd, bebloodied surgeons, dashing about with their instruments and washing themselves over and over. A real surgeon then looked in and cried out, "You guys must be crazy." To which Groucho grinned back, "That's what they said about Pasteur." Today's Andy Warhol may be tomorrow's Bouguereau, perhaps is already today's Bouguereau. I once overheard a literature professor justifying some ephemeral and now-forgotten novel he had chosen for his course by claiming that it was "a Jewish *Wuthering Heights.*" As T.E. Hulme once remarked, works of art aren't eggs.

Industrial artifacts are. They grow stale and, if they didn't, the economy would come to a halt; the Volkswagen Company's refusal to go in for annual changes of style seriously disturbed Detroit. The latest mode of art is not necessarily superior to a previous version, and to study it in universities as though it were is to pay court to science again.

What would happen if it were found that Titian had really copied the work of another artist, unknown till now? The liberal arts professor is entangled in this net of contemporaneity. If innovation is of prime importance, if the artist must invariably produce something new in the manner of the auto manufacturer, then, in the first place, the most eccentric and innovative art (the slags of cement by the New Jersey Turnpike) will always be authenticated and, in the second, we shall be obliged to call a host of masterpieces of the past (all those Madonnas) reprehensible. Finally, if the liberal arts professor claims that his curriculum is valid because it "reflects the times," or gives some other form of "relevance," we must reply that everything reflects the times, including works of totally different content from those he has preferred. Including, also, himself.

Criteria of any serious sort appear to have deserted the liberal arts curriculum. We have reached the point when total insignificance no longer matters on your reading list so long as the students "get involved," "relate to," "dig," and the rest of the lexicon of cant catchphrases that disguise self-expression and self-admiration in an enigmatic paraphrase of what is barely one part of art. Such is the hubris of our liberal curriculum.

Liberation:
Opening the Gates

6
Open Admissions

"Dana can't make himself Easy without he goes to Harvard College," wrote Artemus Ward in 1787. The ideal of allowing everyone to go to college is unexceptionable and unexceptional. If you believe in public education through high school, that is, up to what is now adulthood, it is logical to see easy access to college as an extension of this ideal; and, in fact, no one in his or her senses does oppose open admission to American municipal colleges. Midwestern state universities have long held the concept.

It has, however, lately become something of an educational red herring; the first thing a television interviewer asks you is, Are you for open admission? As well to ask, Are you for the human race? Even William Buckley has come out for open admissions. Criticize in any way the riper idiocies of what is happening in civic education in America and you will be dismissed under the rubric, Oh, I see, you're against open admissions. You are a troglodyte. This tactic sidesteps the true issue, namely, the manner in which open admissions have been administered. Also, the price.

Ideally, everyone ought to be educated and in some countries everyone is. In Paris there used to be free entry to college for anyone with a high school *bac.* Open admissions to

CUNY began in September 1970, after racial rioting had closed City College itself for the third spring in succession, President Gallagher had resigned, and the Board of Higher Education put up its hands and expressed commitment to free higher education for all high school graduates in the city. Initiated in an atmosphere of academic hysteria, at the pistol point of, as we have seen, obscenity and abuse from many who were not students at all, but simply itinerant agitators on loan, the program was without those geographical safeguards which made California's somewhat similar system faintly feasible, and it failed grotesquely to look around any corners.

The basic idea was pretty well-known: if you go on educating people you improve them, and you improve their chances in life, notoriously in an accreditation society. In 1830 the Boston Working Men's Party declared its objective to be "the establishment of a liberal system of education attainable by all." Twenty-two years later Massachusetts passed our first state compulsory school attendance law (twelve weeks of school a year for those between the ages of eight and fourteen). Men like Gallagher and Bowker of New York City clearly saw themselves in the forefront of this tradition. Unfortunately, while it may or may not be true that you improve people by educating them, it is not the case today in America that you automatically send up their job expectancies. The studies coming in are presenting a dim prospect for the college-educated, are indeed, in some cases, showing no evidence of the need for a further four years in what have become, in our big cities, semi-custodial institutions for the unemployable whom you are annually making more so. These facts have to be faced; they cannot be written off as so much reaction. Fourteen American Presidents had less formal education than we today require of a construction worker. None of them did worse than Richard Nixon.

You tend to succeed at school because you have certain qualities, or acquire them, not because you went to school But it is very difficult to get anything approaching this conception into the heads of power-hungry educational politicians. By the time you have done so they will have resigned and be whooping up other tax dollars for the same story elsewhere. Back in the fifties New York City devised the plan of assigning "difficult" pupils to special "600" schools, where they were collected, counseled, recounseled, motivated, encouraged, commiserated with, told how horrible and unfair America was, and so forth. The "600" schools began to proliferate wildly, fattening on the expelled. The Principal of one such school, which was spectacularly vandalized, threw out several hundred pupils *en masse*. The Mayor simply told him to take them all back again—and built more schools. It was the same with open admissions. More education is seen as the only panacea.

Moreover, despite the hoopla, the New York scheme was far less innovative than then-Chancellor Bowker liked to claim. Many state universities (Minnesota in the van) had long admitted any high school graduate. Nor was it so altruistically responsive to student opinion as Bowker liked to represent. The revolutionaries who sat around the table in their melo-dramatic shades "negotiating" with our President were marginal students at best and barely knew what they were initiating, or how. Just—open the doors. Take it from there. And pay later.

Furthermore, it soon became questionable that the program was serving the city's minority youth at all. Remedial classes began to include sizable proportions of Panamanians, Trinidadians, Haitians, people with but the faintest connection with America (when they weren't outright illegal aliens), because news of the bonanza soon got South. I can testify that one colleague that first term had a group of Panamanian girls in his Basic Writing course who were so abusive, stupid, and hostile that he could conduct his classes only by ignoring their presence, as they sulked in the back with their babies. Puerto Ricans, meanwhile, demanded extra credit for having to learn the lingua franca of English in the first place. Nonresident CUNY students are supposed to pay fees, but very few of them do. The penalty might be deportation, after due appeal, but deportation with an American degree is not much hardship for some of these.

Despite the fact, then, that a lenient eye largely overlooked even the high school-diploma requirement that first year, and that the system then bent over backward by giving all freshmen a one-year grace period, *flunking none,* ten thousand freshmen—double the average—dropped out after the first year (ten years after California's master plan got under way only 46% of its freshman class was continuing in college). This is rather expensive. At CUNY, too, grading became so politically friendly as to be risible. One faculty member was quoted in *LC Reporter* (a then faculty organ) as follows:

> To keep faith with our promise to these kids—that we'd give them a fair chance to make it in college instead of cynically proving to them that they can't—we're watering down our standards. Out of guilt for not teaching them properly (23 in a remedial English course!), we're keeping them in college artificially.

Four years later, as City College graduated its first open enrollees, the Chairman of the Board of Higher Education, Alfred A. Giardino, confessed, "Open admissions solved the political issues on which it began, but it has not fully solved the educational issues." In 1976 it failed.

What are the facts? They are hard to get at, since the agency emitting such data is the one concerned to prove itself right. The box score is of its own devising. It is like the statistical juggling that goes on when a hospital wants to show a low number of deaths, and so omits ME (Medical Examiner) fatalities, only to include the latter when it wishes to show a high proportion for other purposes. But in liberal education it is worse, and you are virtually dealing with statistical hoodlums, since it cannot be allowed to be said that open admissions have failed and turned out to be the biggest educational hoax ever perpetrated on the children of the city: say this and you will be witch-hunted out with the zeal of the Inquisition under the banner of another talismanic term, *backlash* (=any idea that disagrees with yours). The Humpty Dumpties of city education can make anything mean what they say it means.

But when the BHE (Board of Higher Education) first started emitting dismaying data concerning open admissions, the liberals bayed back that it was too early to decide. And if the statistics persisted in proving you wrong, you had recourse to some variety of that comment made by Professor Marilyn Gittel, head of CUNY's WAC (Women's Advisory Committee), that "the depth of the problem won't be understood by statistics." You added that the fault was not yours, but society's. Early recognizing that many of these students "do not want to be in college" and have "seeming apathy toward learning," Ms. Mina Shaughnessy, the Circe of CCNY's remedial English program, excused such misfits as "unmotivated," adding, "the problem of the unmotivated student lies outside college—in a labor market that uses the BA indiscriminately to screen applicants."

In fact, remediation (to be studied in the next chapter) soon became a crucial problem. If in English it was chaotic enough, in Math chaos was come again. According to Professor Ralph Kopperman, who headed the first remedial Math program at CCNY (and again I cite only *pro*-open admissions sources), 40% of the remediating students failed to receive passing grades for any course they were in. That's close to half. Kopperman stated: "Many students who come in under Open Admissions have never had any high school Math. They were given something called Business Math and that's only arithmetic." Yet he observed: "So while we can't be considered an overwhelming success, nor are we a failure." There used to be a Carlsberg beer ad showing a glass half full of beer—or was it half empty? You were either an optimist or a pessimist. The same sophism came out at this time from CUNY Chancellor Robert J. Kibbee: "I have to look at the class being 71% full after the first year rather than 29% empty." The reasoning is too absurd to bear discussion.

Why did not students in high school get much more than cash-register or bank-teller arithmetic? A typical New York City high school has a *daily* absentee rate of 30%. Our fault, of course, for nonmotivation. There are times, of course, when I can hardly blame these kids for choosing the candy store rather than the classroom as a warm place to be; the gross square feet per CUNY student has now been assessed as 74 (that of SUNY being 212). You do far better in Nedick's of a morning.

Four years after City College had initiated so-called open admissions, it graduated precisely 110 students among a total of 3,687 who, according to its new President, would not have been let in under the previous admissions policy. President Marshak hailed this slender and costly achievement as making "free higher education in this city broader and richer than ever before." The figure meant that only a little over 10% of the students allowed in four years before with previously unacceptable admissions criteria had graduated. Proponents, with Marshak prominent among them, began to cite and publish letters of glowing gratitude from graduates who would not have been under old standards. But the *New*

York Times continued, through September 1974, to publish retention rate tables, the most optimistic of which showed a CUNY dropout rate of close on 50%.

Consisting of eight senior colleges and ten two-year community colleges, CUNY had previously published its own report on "Student Retention under Open Admissions." It was ostensibly an optimistic document (the educators concerned might lose their jobs if it wasn't) but, when coldly scrutinized by our Professional Staff Congress (AFT-NEA), it revealed astonishing lacunae. Forty-seven percent of the open admissions students admitted in September 1970 had dropped out enroute—in fact, after only two years of so-called study (CUNY had claimed here a figure of but 30%). PSC showed statistical techniques, or mere legerdemain, by means of which CUNY had exaggerated retention rates of such students. Two thousand ninety-nine of this sort were simply missing, somewhere.

Moreover, retention under the lenient grading and almost total-forgiveness standards instanced in the *New York Times* hardly meant very much. Doubtless the statistics will go on being swapped, but they will not signify, since Mr. Giardino's comment is all-operative. Open admissions is a juicy political plum. If it has resulted in an ethnic transformation of the second largest institution of higher education in the United States, it cannot be far wrong. New York's mammouth CUNY complex, which had grown from 172,726 in 1969 to 259,374 by the fall of 1973, was repeating what had happened in California, but neither system could be politically faulted. What students and faculty themselves thought about it was beside the point. A poll of our senior class, taken in 1972 by our Department of Student Personnel Services, showed nearly half opposed to open admissions (these were *students*, mind). As for the faculty, who were trying to cope with the mess and wondering whether CUNY was becoming the senior class of Rikers Island rather than that Open Sesame promised to the underprivileged, Professor Belle Zeller, Hunter College Math teacher and Chairwoman of CUNY's Legislative Conference, put it plainly in this same year:

> The faculty, which threw itself whole-heartedly into the Open Admissions program, is becoming demoralized by the obstacles in its path, and more and more students who have displayed remarkable patience with those obstacles are telling me of their growing suspicion that Open Admissions is now a fraud.

In face of such numbers, how may one talk about *so-called* open admissions? Why, because they are only partially open. You still have to have a high school diploma to get into one of the New York or California higher colleges. Is not this elitist? Surely it would be more democratic to scrap even that standard. One day it will be conceived to be, by the next round of pseudo-revolutionaries with their clenched fists and "Right on's."

The taxpayer will be told he has to pay for any Tom, Dick or Harry who strays off the street in search of a warm corner near a radiator in winter and doze away a lecture on how to make Zen candlesticks, from which he will awake with an A. Deafening applause at graduation. I honestly cannot see why high school averages or graduation should by current logic be allowed to impede anyone. And this will simply create a new elite. As Anthony Burgess pointed out in an article in the *New York Times Magazine*, turning our urban universities into "glorified high schools" will simply be to provoke into emergence "superuniversities," where serious study can be done. After them will come "supersuperuniversities" ever more and more remote from the national life. "More has meant worse," wrote Kingsley Amis in a justly celebrated polemic. "Student unrest has several causes, but here and now the prime one seems to me to be the presence in our universities of an academically unfit majority, or large minority." More and more mass education means less and less true higher education; this is the inescapable fact.

The problem then remains that, if the survival rate of open admissions students is so low, even with few requirements and hyperfriendly grades, do they really want to be there? This is the gut issue. No one dare reply in the negative, since this would be acknowledging the defeat of your motive ideal. It would be to undermine your own certainties. After all, you don't see two experts arguing on television, with one of them suddenly throwing up his hands and saying, "Yes, yes, you're right. I've been hopelessly mistaken all my life." But if mass education is your messiah, then you have to have masses coming to be educated; and, in this respect, what is happening in America has, for a variety of reasons, already happened in Sweden. In the course of the sixties Swedish universities mushroomed from an intake of eight to thirty thousand. Then came their disruptions, mild by our standards. After these the enrollment sank back in a few years to twenty-three thousand. College teaching jobs became hard, if not impossible, to get. And those who got them were not likely to rock the boat.

In America, however, it is difficult to reverse a growth rate without feeling guilty somewhere along the line, since the industrial civilization itself is predicated on expansion. From 1940 to 1970 our college enrollments grew from about one and a half million to eight and a half million. It is correct, if not pleasant, to point out that the first major slackening in such enrollments began when draft-dodging via college ("seeking academic sanctuary")* was no longer necessary, in the late sixties.

---

*As Jacques Barzun observed, the students who were squealing for "Sanctuary!" were also screaming "Down with Alma Mater!"

But now, also for a variety of reasons, the college-age population appears to have peaked out numerically, and soon it will be in decline. Hence it seems likely that ever-increasing and ever-widening egalitarianism will become, in the eighties, the only answer to the implicit criticism of college desertion. Already we have seen city systems virtually holding their students in college in order to prove their vast new bureaucratic apparati right. In a taxpayer-supported situation, egalitarianism is always going to make potent political appeal and thus win out over something dubbed as elitism, which heresy will soon be able to be indulged in by only a tiny minority of independent institutions. For the municipal teacher this means—let us make no mistake about it—back to kindergarten. My student Tyrone, sitting in a half-lotus pose in back of class with a transistor strapped to his Afro, and nodding off every two minutes, is going to be a city teacher's dream by comparison with what will be occupying his seat in 1984.

At the moment egalitarianism at the urban multiversity means ethnicity. In CUNY minority-group enrollment supposedly grew from 18.8 in 1969 (prior to open admissions, a far higher figure being used by Gallagher at the time) to 35.6% in 1973; the general public is seldom aware that such percentages are wholly factitious, since by law no student is obliged to state his or her race, such data being voluntarily offered on an IBM card. Self-designation is notoriously unreliable and becoming more so, we shall see, as people find themselves being pushed around by agencies like HEW (Health, Education and Welfare). A whole group at Michigan, for instance, wrote themselves down as American Indians. One applicant for a federal post put down Black under the voluntary *Race?* question; when a supervisor remonstrated with him in person, since he was evidently

White, he was met with the deserved retort, "You don't know my mother."

When it comes to these so-called minority groups, everyone surrenders. Here is Irving Howe, a Hunter English Professor, at the end of a peroration enveighing against the condescension implicit in lowered standards:

> There remains an important problem concerning the relationship between minority subcultures, racial and/or ethnic, and the dominant culture that we call Western. Some academics are content with the formalism of a seemingly unimpeachable stand: they applaud "equality of opportunity," they will receive qualified students of any race, creed, or color, and they propose to bend neither backward nor forward. This view, despite its seeming liberalism, neglects the crucial fact that anything like equality of opportunity is impossible when the circumstances of competing groups are so radically different, indeed, when socio-cultural deprivations are so deeply ingrained that formal equality of opportunity may have little effect but to perpetuate existing inequalities of condition.

This is pleasantly written, has a persuasively resonant ring, but to anyone who has taught within a multiracial city system for a quarter of a century or more, it is still so much balderdash.

The safeguarding of standards in the interests of a viable society is said to neglect "the crucial fact that anything like equality of opportunity is impossible when the circumstances of competing groups are so radically different." Let us translate, or de-euphemize, this: it says, in effect, that Black students have quite exceptional deprivations within urban high schools. But so do Jews, so do Asiatics, both of whom study, and succeed, alongside them, in the same "ghetto" classrooms. (It is an irony that the term *ghetto*, originally the Jewish quarter of a city, has been purloined for almost wholly

Black purposes in our dialogue today.) Nor is the difference between sexes emphasized, George Pettitt telling us, in *Prisoners of Culture*, that young females in our schools are "as much as two years farther along on the road to maturity" than young males of the same age. Black students are by now spread all over the high school network of New York City. These schools have notoriously low standards throughout, the reading skills of their denizens falling well below the national average (54.1% so classified in 1965 growing to 66.2% in 1971).

Howe is typical of the more decent kind of liberal; his intellectual conscience will not let him say that when you lower a standard it still remains what it was before, but his emotional socialism has to leave some loophole for "socio-cultural deprivations." Leonard Kriegel, whose book has been mentioned above, is of the same stamp; he writes an eloquent exposé of the horrors of teaching at City College but shies away, at the end of it, from any real indictment of the root causes. The hell of our city colleges is paved with these good intentions and one owes it to the "ghetto kids" to fight this mind as one fights the devil, without rest and without quarter.

Flipping through IBM cards to gather statistics, the liberal of this type cannot really "see" the Black. He has already decided that every college-age student of this race has come from a ghetto. The equation often but not always obtains (Nigerians, Ugandans?); the liberal cannot see the individual Black as a person, since part of his nature requires to envisage him, first and foremost, as an educational digit to fit into a slot in order to prove a political point. I have had Blacks in my classes who had complete contempt for the current lack of standards, and for the balding, bearded guerrillas with tenure who misadminister them. This sense was reflected, too, in comments quoted in the *New York Times* by our first graduating open admissions students.

Finally, as regards this deep ingraining of crippling differences that Howe mentions, the Coleman/Johns Hopkins Report found that in the mid-sixties the educational opportunities for Blacks and Whites were actually about the same; money spent on each probably favored Blacks. Teacher potentialities in Black and White schools were roughly the same (*Equality of Educational Opportunity*, Washington, D.C.: U.S. Government Printing Office, 1966, Prepared by James S. Coleman et al.). The Coleman Report even found that Black children did best when in *mixed* schools, a confutation of our newly segregated ethnic studies and one devoutly to be hushed (though Roy Wilkins of NAACP challenged Black compulsory segregation as vigorously as he had earlier fought White). But say "sociocultural deprivations" to Congress and, like Pavlov's dog, it will salivate money. How many of these programs are remembered five years later is a moot point. Not so long ago Congress churned educational cash into something called Head Start; this is now better known as a men's scalp formula.

Occasionally the cruder kind of educator, intent on producing rapid results rather than examining causes in the manner of an Irving Howe, will be caught rigging the deck or loading the dice. The Anti-Defamation League of the B'nai B'rith began investigating just how openly admitted were the students of City College's Center for Biomedical Education; it did so in response to complaints from high school students who claimed to be better qualified than those eventually admitted into the program.

President Marshak used another slide rule for the openness of his admissions here, admitting that "Blacks and Hispanics were often given higher ratings than White students on the categories of maturity and commitment." High school students with averages of 94-97 who found themselves rejected in favor of those with lower scores presumably lacked "maturity and commitment."

How anyone determined this in a short interview in which some candidates later said they had been asked no questions testing these qualities at all remained a mystery. What you do find out in even a quick interview, of course, is skin color. The final breakdown of 39.7% White and 60.3% minority was a significant alteration of the 50/50 ratio of the recommended applicants. And when you examined the application tables more closely you saw even clumsier loadings: among the applicants recommended by the Admissions Committee for acceptance were six Asian males, of whom two were accepted, and ten Latin males, of whom ten were accepted. Despite this gross loading on its own behalf, our Black student paper was not in the slightest mollified, writing, "A final example of White reality is the Bio-Medical Program that was sold by the mind of Robert Marshak to the funding fathers as a means of attracting *higher quality White students* back to City College. . . .the dehumanizing educational process will drive out many students of color."

When you have lived through open admissions, you come to realize that they will never be open enough. California is the apparent pioneer and paragon of public higher education. It admits—and how it can physically do more I do not know—three ranks of high school graduates based on school scores and SAT tests (in New York it used to be the Regent's exam). Rank One goes to the university, Rank Two to one of the state colleges, Rank Three to one of the junior colleges. This operation, now being increasingly deserted, was then found nonegalitarian and discriminatory since, as in New York, there were clusters of Blacks in the lower echelons. At the university Blacks still only formed less than 1%, and less than 3% in the state colleges. An ex-Chancellor of the State Colleges of California called it unfair; Blacks were being penalized "because the lower schools had not adequately prepared them for academic success," adding that "that unfairness was defended in the name of 'standards' and 'equal opportunity on the basis of achievement.' "

So you are back to Square One. What are you going to reward for, please, if not achievement? Misachievement? You call the system "meritocracy" and "segregation" and you accuse the delinquent educators concerned of, virtually speaking, not actually lifting minority students into class seats by their Afros and keeping them there with automatic A's. You keep on expanding your numbers until it is impossible, in the words of historian D. C. Watt, "even to give the extra students the same standard of attention enjoyed by their existing students." You turn once-proud public colleges into what Charles Frankel calls "holding institutions for people past seventeen."

When open admissions became the order of the day at CUNY in 1970, it was clearly physically impossible to admit every high school graduate into one of the four tax-supported colleges (City, Hunter, Brooklyn, Queens). Hence a certain sorting-out based on capabilities had to take place; it is remarkable, indeed, and a tribute to our overworked registrars, that wholesale anarchy did not prevail. But the result was again dubbed meritocracy. Some applicants were sorted "down" to the community colleges, under the auspices of what was called a "tracking" system. These colleges again showed high Black enrollment ratios. Buell Gallagher writes:

> The resulting *de facto* segregation within the City University, despite the fact that blacks make up 22 percent of the total undergraduate enrollment, has not been corrected by open admissions.*

If you follow this line, and it will be institutionalized by the eighties, you will echo that *de facto* to the rafters. For you

---

*One must again enter a **caveat** or caution concerning the confidence with which these percentages are given; they can only be approximate since by law no student has to state his or her race.

can't *force* minority students into the desired top 12%. All you can do, to prove your social theories right, is to break the rules in the manner of a Marshak and put them there by impalpables like *maturity* and *commitment*. As Mayor Karl Luger of Vienna used to declare, "I myself decide who is a Jew." A Dies Irae is undoubtedly coming for public education in this sector. Already the lawsuits are piling up. Whatever you do you are elitist. So lower absolutely everything and score simply by hue and gender. We shall meet CUNY's "visual" identification of applicants below.

If you are going to evaluate in *any* way, there are bound to be some who will end up at the bottom of the class; by IQ standards of twenty years ago only 25% of the present college-age population have the 110 IQ then requisite for college attendance. In this sense Princeton's Fritz Machlup seems justified in calling *universal higher education** "simply a contradiction in terms." For to be higher you must be superior to someone else; Machlup proposes that we should perhaps call what is going on *longer* education; certainly a concept of longer or broader education in open admissions would be more charitable to the less gifted, rather than arousing their hopes by other terminology. "What the college has created," writes Ernest van den Haag, "is ambition untethered to possibility—an unhappy person who is likely to hold society responsible for his frustration and who, therefore, will be harmful to it." Another way, in short, in which academe goes about its own assassination. This took place in 1976.

It is conceivable that our public colleges will one day devise an examination system whereby you take only the failures into the free colleges. In 1984 those with scores over

---

*The phrase is taken from the Gardner Task Force Report of 1964, which served as the basis of the Higher Education Act of 1965.

ninety will, it may be argued, get by in life well enough. We owe them nothing. "Reparations" must be paid, however, to those with scores under sixty; *we* have failed *them* in not providing adequate preparation at the high and junior high and elementary school levels. And if you *still* come out of this exercise with more Whites than Blacks in the classroom, even though the latter form barely eleven percent of the population, why pretend? Count skins.

But this infraction of all rules has to be another treachery. Forcing the democrat to be undemocratic, it is yet another kind of intellectual hara-kiri. You have to sterilize part of your mind to accomplish it. To call in the Yahoos, with their slogans and placards, and then spout joyous lies at them seems some sort of ultimate in academic self-immolation.

7

Remediation

Adult illiteracy, like child abuse, is a subject on which emotions grow fierce. There are two million adult illiterates even today in England, and that is measuring by a reading age of the average nine-year-old. The UNESCO standard is of the average thirteen-year-old. By it a considerable percentage, probably a majority, of the City University of New York would be classed as illiterate. As Nicholas von Hoffman once neatly put it, "half the population is under twenty-five, but half of them are under twelve." A CCNY counselor, Dr. Richard Soll, concedes that "almost one-third of those entering fall into the category of needing two or more remedial courses." But here emotions boil and to fail any of these individuals is tantamount to infanticide. If CUNY enrolls a student it will move hell and high water not to let him go, in order to prove the politicians right, despite the fact that remediation itself discloses that you are pushing into higher education those who simply do not have the requisite skills.

The politicians in our midst have, in fact, now ordained that remediation shall henceforth be known as *compensation*, presumably for past injustices and deprivations. This fiat is a curious one. It is particularly political since it says that the illiterates who arrive at our registration tables are not so much deprived as oppressed. As in the expectation of the famous Brazilian educator Paulo Freire, literacy will happen directly you understand the nature of your oppression. Many of our Basic Writing courses seem to operate on this principle, teaching more about the injustices of society outside the classroom than the use of punctuation within it. The command is curious, too, since I cannot recall its having been applied to the generations of Asiatic or Jewish students who have passed beneath my gaze: the children of the Hiroshima holocaust and the concentration camps surely cry out for "compensation" rather more than the victims of another context and century, a time when eight-year-old White girls were still going down mines.

Remediation (as I propose to call it here, since that is what it is) has become one of the principal problems of the Open Admissions concept. Money is thrown at it recklessly. In operations like our university's SEEK, or our English Department's inflated Basic Writing courses, you can see the old, self-perpetuating routine of creating yet one more program on the backs of the taxpayers.

Hordes of new teachers are hired, all professing to have the key to remediation (Black English, Visual Thinking); they then pour out a steady stream of articles and statistics purporting to prove the success of what they are teaching, stances not always unmotivated by the desire to retain their jobs. The programs are indeed doomed to succeed because the teacher is always wrong and the student always right. "I do know," writes Ann Petrie, "that if the promise of Open Admissions has failed them, it was not their fault." She goes on to reassure herself: "Basic Writing has to be one of the finest remedial programs in all of CUNY. It has dynamic leadership, a well designed progression of classes; a Writing Center; a core of dedicated teachers." Why, then, is it so little working that she is forced in the same breath to confess, "At the end of four months, four class hours a week, and sometimes as much again in conference and tutoring at the Writing Center, verb endings were still incorrect, words were still misspelled, subjects still did not agree with verbs"?

Is it just possible that many of these students are being virtually compelled to attend these higher colleges? With so little respect for the educational environment—Hunter quintupling its enrollment in three years and bursting into nearby office space while our own "facilities" groan at the seams— the new student scarcely bothers to attend and gets aggrieved, often belligerent, when you drop him for coming to only a couple of classes or so. (After all, he has come from a high school system where, on any given day, one-third don't show up for class.) Ms. Petrie tells a tearjerker of one woman who failed to attend regularly and "who invented one health reason after another, headaches to brain tumor, to explain her absences. It was not until the middle of the semester that I learned her real problem was a year-old, asthmatic child. She was not married and embarrassed to tell me." Again, the flaws in this story are all too obvious; where college fails, home must be at fault. You are conveniently relieved of responsibility, or lying.

A professional counselor to Open Admissions students in our DSPS (Department of Student Personnel Services), Rod Hill, says: "We've tried many approaches. We've invited students in for appointments, set up groups such as Freshman orientation, tried forcing students to come in by holding up their registration. But none of these things has made for continued contact." To which, presumably, the dedicated knee-jerk liberal would simply shrug that if you save only a single one of these souls it's worth the $30 million of taxpayers' money that the City of New York allocated in extra aid in reading, writing, and arithmetic for underprepared college students in 1974.

I must admit that I would feel bitter were I a Jewish student of the past, holding the same degree that the lady with the asthmatic illegitimate has now obtained gratis, and to whom none of these especial forgivenesses and latitudes was given. Every now and then SUNY threatens, via legislative action, to take over the CUNY system. All work stops while busloads of students and faculty rush up to Albany to protest the proposal, which might mean that the city colleges would begin to charge fees. At present writing, the latest mitigation presented by the (originally Rockefeller-led) wing in the state capitol assured all concerned that abundant scholarship support would be available to minority students. The answer thrown back was, again, Unfair! Why so? Well, it was said, such students would never pick up their scholarship checks. One can only say that if you are too lazy to pick up a check not to have sit in a class in order to be given a degree, you deserve to get one at birth. The motto of our administration could be summarized as follows: "We don't know what's going on, but we're certain it is. And anyway, the City will pay for it."

Belle Zeller, President of the CUNY Professional Staff Congress (AFT-NEA), claims that "remediation has not been adequately administered." CCNY Linguistics Professor Louis Heller says it has failed: "They are not coming out of remediation with the skills they are supposed to have." But they will continue to go in, just so long as you treat education as political psychotherapy—and the City remains solvent. For it is a feature of the liberal invariably to know better than everyone else—about sex, race, religion, as well as education. Our present President has been completely disloyal from the start to everything City College has stood for during a century, but his conception has to be ours, or else. *Cuius regio, eius religio.*

Confront a liberal with the facts above, that despite everything being done to make the classroom a place of entertainment, the new students are not attending the classes, and you receive the response: That's because we haven't properly motivated them. Yet this assumes that *you* know what should be someone's (true, real, inner) motives better than they do. "Patronize and you perish," cries my present Chairman, in an article published in *Change* magazine. But surely this is the grossest form of patronage. It derives from the irritation: Dammit, they ought to be in college, I know they ought to be, but for some reason they don't want to be.

Years and years of political schooling rather than education have produced this result. You have set Johnny to read his racist writers, publicly honored Malcolm X and Eldridge Cleaver. Little wonder when Johnny gives you, at college level, the thick jeer—Why should I take Whitey Math and Whitey Physics, to enter a Whitey world? Haven't you just proved to me that The Man will never let me get ahead? A guideline for referral to our Division of Counseling and Psychological Services before me asks classroom faculty "to recognize signals that indicate that a student is experiencing emotional problems which warrant help." Among these:

> If the student is apathetic, detached or unresponsive
> If the student misses several classes and is erratic in attendance
> If the student sleeps in class. . . .

I share the contempt a young "ghetto kid" must feel for the mind behind this document, and others like it. Can it really be as easy as this? Can you spit at a professor, revile him daily in class, and still get a pat on the back plus an affectionate A? How ludicrous can these liberals get? My Chairman, Edward Quinn, went on in his article:

> I recall the student in the back of my class, during a discussion of *Troilus and Cressida,* holding up a sign that read: LANGUAGE SUCKS. Did I throw him out on his ear as some of my colleagues would have done a few years earlier? No, I listened to the

explanation: when measured against the transcendental, mystical experience of the absolute vouchsafed to one who had tripped on acid and seen God, language—even Shakespeare's—did indeed suck.

Only occasionally does our professoriat gag on such arrogance: a year or so ago, one of our student evaluation handbooks published a collection of comments by some of the undergraduates on their instructors. When the latter were ladies, these became specific—"Big tits. . .good boobs, would make a great lay," etc.—and the ladies' ire was aroused. Here feminism could be called into the fray.

Another way of shelving the remedial problem is to refer the blame to the high schools. They then shift it onto junior high, whence it goes into the home. This is *you*. You are guilty for that ghetto home and must remediate and compensate for it as rapidly as possible. If in this task an A for absence will help, it is entirely excusable. And yet there are a lot of Jewish kids in those same ghetto schools, and they aren't squealing. I think of the by now thousands of Jewish boys and girls who have passed before me from far harder homes and lives than those of most Blacks in Harlem today—in fact, not infrequently flung out of those homes for daring to want to go on getting educated instead of helping split packing cases in Solly's grocery. No air-conditioning, constant TV, only the latest baby bawling away while you tried to master Calc. And you did.

What, too, of Asiatics with even sterner problems, notably the primal one of language? Chinese is another language group altogether and its speakers have to exert great diligence simply to get by in English. I remember a Chinese family in a grossly ghetto apartment of the mid-fifties who sent two sons to City College, and to Yale Ph.D.'s thereafter. Both are in high-paying jobs now. But the excuses must forever be made, even apparently for the junkie. Ex-CCNY President Buell Gallagher writes, "A twenty-year-old in Harlem says he shoots horse because he can't stand the smell of urine in the stairwell and the stink of garbage in the kitchen." Whose urine is this, by the way, and whose garbage?

Yet another patch put on the crazy quilt of our errors in education in this area is bilingualism. In January 1974 the Supreme Court ruled unanimously that San Francisco's schools must provide special classes for Chinese-speaking children, on the grounds that to be able to speak Chinese only was an impediment to learning that constitutes discrimination on the basis of national origin. The California school system contains four million children and officially admits that there are today nearly a quarter of a million with next to no English or actually none at all. This, by inference, is then said to be our fault. Since America has not annexed China—yet—one assumes that most of these Chinese speakers arrived on the continent in a voluntary fashion. I suggest they try demanding costly special instruction by Chinese-speaking teachers when they immigrate to France.

America has been quite astonishingly generous in this matter and New York City, of course, is currently moving to require Spanish for teacher certification. Why, then, should those who teach in Yorkville not be made to speak German? Illinois, Massachusetts, and Texas now all require bilingual instruction for non-English-speaking pupils. The implications have hardly yet been sounded out. Compelling cities to have translators beside voting booths is simply an admission that those voters are unable to evaluate the political platforms on offer. If it is relatively hard to find Portuguese-speaking teachers for Portuguese-speaking children, and Tagalog-speaking instructors for those from the Philippines, you plead for federal funding for a new "project" in the field. And you contribute thereby to the death wish for what you are really saying in this capitulation is that America is *inferior* to the country of origin. We must learn your language, not you ours.

A final method for eluding criticism in this area is to continue or collaborate with the going lunacy. This is now done not in the spirit of the Mad Hatter but on the level of Deans. About half of our entering freshpeople each term now take some remedial Math courses. A Math Lab spawned sixty-five new teachers over two semesters, and its administrator has, as I write, just sent in a whopping new request for tutors' salaries. Yet still the flunk rate rises.

The first answer to this is to complain to the program's director (a Professor Tse), blame the teachers and, as in China, sit on any dissenters among them:

> If any student gets angry enough to complain in writing to Tse, the complaint is investigated and acted upon. Once a student complained that a tutor refused to explain something, saying that it was clear to any third-grader, and he then went on to denounce the whole remedial program, calling its students "stupid." He was fired.*

Such is one solution. Another seems to be to say that even Math is unnecessary these days. In "Do They Have To Know Math?" Morton F. Kaplon, a Mathematics Professor and also a Dean at City College, proposes that, because "the typewriter has outmoded the need for good penmanship, and our curriculum has recognized that," high-speed computers and the like have largely done away with the need for Math for our sort of students. "Our attitudes in a legal sense towards homosexuality, drugs, capital punishment and many other 'crimes' have changed significantly. Society has agreed that things have changed. Cannot our attitude towards what we

---

*From an article in CCNY student newspaper **Observation Post**.

agree to call a college education also change?" Or even a standard, for that matter. Why bother if our surgeon extracts a kidney instead of an appendix?

The thalidomide tragedy, to which thousands of living victims daily testify, was caused by lack of customary scientific rigor. The first atom bomb was dropped as a result of mistranslation; after the Allied ultimatum demanding unconditional surrender, the Japanese Premier used the term *mokusatsu* to characterize his country's reply. It was understood by both cabinet and himself as meaning "taking no action at present." A news agency translated it as rejection. The worst air disaster to date was the crash of a DC 10 outside Paris, in March 1974, due to the fact that an illiterate loader couldn't read the instructions about closing the hatch. Dean Kaplon would presumably reply that soon computers will do this for him, anyway. "Why," asks this $45,000-a-year administrator, "do we insist that they all have some defineable level of competence in arithmetic operations when we have readily available the modern counterpart of the typewriter (as a substitute for penmanship) in the miniature electronic calculator?" He goes blithely on, "Why do we insist that there exist some common standard of prose for communication when we have available the tape recorder to record and transmit the words we say?" This is the ultimate condescension; it implies that all the Math or English our students are going to need in society is that of a bank teller, supermarket checker, or gas jerk. So why worry?

Math is empirical. English is judgmental. There is no stigma involved in telling me I am hopeless at logarithms and a total duffer at the chain rule. There is in telling a twenty-year-old with two children and a wife on welfare that he can't communicate in English. Whose English? Dean Kaplon is right. In the society he and his kind have organized, English is an effete and contaminated language, a vehicle for imperialism. In 1974 the Conference on College Composition and Communications (known in the trade as the 4C's) solemnly voted "to uphold the right of students to their own language."

"Their own language" does not appear to be much of a contract. In the fall of 1974 nearly half the freshpersons at the University of California at Berkeley failed an easy English composition examination. At the University of Houston at this time 60% of all freshpersons failed the first three essays they wrote. Similarly tested in the same semester, one Harvard student lamented, "I tried to write what I was really feeling and I got all these irrelevant comments about grammar all over the pages. I ran through the streets of Cambridge weeping." It is we who should be doing the weeping, and will be tomorrow.

It is not for critics to try to unscramble these particular eggs. A teacher's job is to teach well, and maintain a high level of pedagogical competence. He has no say in what students may be ranked before him. His loyalty is to his subject. If you don't like the student body allotted you by higher beings, go elsewhere. Drive trucks. But one method devised by city fathers for solving the remediation havoc deserves mention here; it is that of the community college.

In New York City the two-year community college is presently being asked to repair the ravages of miseducation by knife and needle, taking place in the corridors of the average high school. At present, high school graduates in the *lower* half of their class (imagine what that is like!) are taken into the senior colleges as and when space permits; but they are assured admission into a community college. In the latter we now find huge accretions of minority students—91.5% at Hostos, 68.3% at Manhattan Community College. A glance at what goes on at the latter is instructive, since it is expected that by 1980 as much as 40% of what is called higher education in this country will be located in these free or low-cost intermediary colleges. Already California boasts a vast system of these, eventually to be available to everyone of college age within the state, and especially of minority status.

Manhattan Community College is one of ten two-year post-high school institutions within the City University. Funded out of taxes, it enrolls around ten thousand, whom it prepares for the four-year colleges, or to be our nurses, medical technicians, bookkeepers, and so on. Its premises are scattered buildings on the West Side of Manhattan between 48th and 70th streets. Around the doors of these establishments, any evening, hookers push and pushers cruise, as in the infamous Alamac Hotel, a junkies' paradise originally foisted off on CCNY as a dormitory for remediants.

Alas for the Board of Higher Education, the *New York Times* got access to a confidential evaluation of this community college and was stimulated to conduct an investigation of its own. It found that some 70% of the nursing graduates had failed their state exams, that student fees had been used to buy cars for student government leaders or send others on unauthorized trips to Africa, and that Deans out of favor with the big brass were "reassigned to nonfunctional titles," though still earning as much as $40,000 each of the taxpayers' money a year. A faculty committee reported in "pedaguese" that "while monies were improperly expended, pursuit of the situation would not be in the best interests of the overall student body." White Robert Kibbee, Chancellor of CUNY, charged, "the college is chewing on its vitals." His investigative committee found faculty morale at "an all-time low," and student grades "inflated beyond meaning" (a topic I will develop in the next chapter). Black Dr. Edgar Draper, President of Manhattan Community College, replied, "College morale is wonderful."

Manhattan is cited here, not only for its gross misuse of public money, but because it represents a crucial link in the remedial chain. Weak students—particularly those deficient in reading and math—are channeled into the upper civic colleges via the community colleges on the ground that the latter will remedy their deficiencies. Manhattan was accorded a remediation role but refused for its first few years to institute any formal remediation classes. Students reading at sixth-grade level (adult illiterates) registered in courses of their choice. But when Kibbee's evaluation team accused Manhattan of reneging on remediation, Draper's men retorted:

> It should be pointed out that most laymen have a somewhat confused idea of the relationships which exist between reading level and functional abililties. For instance, many jobs in our society (shop attendant, service-station attendant, warehouse-man's assistant, etc.) call for a fourth-grade reading level. And the *New York Times'* news sections are written at a ninth-grade level.

That's telling them.

The community college is the city's *Danegeld* paid to its guilty past: after the revelations cited above Manhattan presented 1,685 degrees inside, appropriately enough, a circus tent at the foot of Chambers Street. The Mayor, the Borough President, and all the highest city education officials dug gold-plated shovels into the earth in front of the dais. A new campus was broken out. Quite how much use all these degrees will be, except as a sop to the educational conscience, is problematical. Finally, Mayor Beame, the commencement speaker, boomed, "Be proud of the fact that you attended Manhattan Community College."

Unfortunately, the sad facts remain. If you spit on education, it will spurn you. If you shirk the duty of hard-core remediation, and shelve the matter as a social welfare problem, to be solved by someone else, your students will give up too. As Marianne Moore put it,

> The student studies
>   voluntarily, refusing to
> be less than individual.

Manhattan College and its kin represent the end of the road in the remediation anomie. Abandon it, let everyone do what he or she likes, fire all critics as racist, and what do you get?

Well, you get a total disruption and standstill of Manhattan College, all paid for by the taxpayer, by a student organization called the Third World Coalition. You get the revelation that this group spent a reserve student government fund of $350,000 on Pontiacs and delegations to political meetings that could be guaranteed to be anti-American.

You cannot lift yourself up by your bootstraps if you insist on cutting them off all the time. This is all a considerable pity since it is still possible, even in Manhattan, to find institutions of education with genuine *esprit de corps*. A year ago I met with students at the High School of Performing Arts. This building is in one of the most unacademic areas of the city, surrounded by pantyhose and porn shops. It has none of the affluence accorded to Dean Mina Rees's 42nd Street Graduate Center. Yet, by its own students, this high school is well kept up. One floor devoted to ballet was impeccable. Obscene graffiti and the drooling junkies of City College corridors were outside on the streets, rather than inside the classrooms. It was a good place to be. Both students and teachers sesemed to believe in what they were doing. And what they were doing was educating.

8
Grading

The evaluation of academic work today summarizes the contradictions of office in which the university teacher is now caught. On one hand, he declines to be a teacher as too authoritarian; even the legal status of *in loco parentis* of the institution itself toward its offspring has now been reversed in the courts, though *in statu pupillari* is insisted on by the same abolitionists when students are confronted by the military or police. On the other hand, the teacher has to grade; the scientific civilization into which his charges are to be given a helping hand demands standards of performance of those intending to operate it. Else this civilization will run even further amok.

As a result of this contradiction, students in a large state or municipal college are likely to find two orders of teachers, those in the sciences who are obliged to test, and grade, and examine, and the new academic swingers of the humanities who increasingly refuse to do so since, they allege, they are not instructing their students so much as sharing experiences with them.

The former group, as Steven Cahn has shown in "The Eclipse of Excellence," are the more democratic; they know that all men are equal before the ineluctability of cosines and decimal points; they sleep well at night, where their *livre de chevet* is Ortega y Gasset's *The Revolt of the Masses* with its memorable instruction, "Barbarism is the absence of standards to which appeal can be made."

It is the second group who get involved in fist fights with students over C's and waste of public money by having to station guards outside their office doors against the aggrieved and frankly menacing (a colleague in the Classics Department recently resigned in the face of death threats by a paranoiac). By now everyone has his or her own horror story of the kind. When I recently failed over half a class in a Basic Writing course, considerable pressure was brought on me to relent: a friend who flunked yet more in Physics One had no such repercussions. When I equally recently failed a graduating senior (Black, female) for total incompetence, my Chairperson sent down an infuriated henchcreature to dissuade me. I stuck to my guns, but if I hadn't had tenure I'd have been fired.

Grading is of course undemocratic. So is a driving test. For its own cohesion, and for the survival of its sidewalk citizens, society is obligated to demand certain standards of accomplishment. Oxbridge did not examine you at all for two or three years (Pass Mods was a joke). A lot of us felt this to be unfair. We wanted to know how we were doing. Also, three exhausting and neurotic weeks of nonstop examinations at the end of the journey did not seem a reasonable procedure, particularly if you were not feeling your best at the time. J. C. Masterman supports the system as follows: "If examinations there must be, then those at Oxford are probably the fairest and most reasonable that can be devised. It seems to me odious to impose on men an examination in which every answer is separately marked and the totals added up in order that each man may be given a place." But while he says this he makes little real justification for the practice; he had not come across the student who came into my office last term, furiously brandishing a blue book and exclaiming, "What's the cream on this garbage, man?" He was referring to the D+I had given him. As Berkeley's Henry F. May has put it, "giving grades to students or denying their right to devise their own education is compared to denying votes to Negroes."

Oxbridge was charged with producing a superior individual. Every argument in the world can today be leveled at this relic, but his standards of success were quite different from those of us living in an American city today. Hundreds of Oxford products barely bothered to look into the remote corners of the *Gazette* to see how they had been graded. Dozens of members of the House of Commons would have refused to submit themselves to a competitive examination. A. E. Housman was "ploughed" at Oxford (not even given, that is, a Fourth, but failed) and he later became the Kennedy Professor of Latin at Cambridge; our approximate equivalents, like R. P. Blackmur, are very rare indeed.

I once knew a Corsican Count whose family had been ennobled in the thirteenth century but who had never troubled to get a driving license. Finally, when he was nearly sixty, the Prefecture sent an agent around to test him; it was an apologetic visit and the Count drove with *panache* about his mountain village, only to end up running straight into the wall of the Gendarmerie. Still shaking, the agent turned to him, "Mon Comte, I will give you your driving license, but you must promise never to drive again." The bargain was honored. At Oxford—and I think at Oxford only, during his short spell there—Einstein used to pretend that he couldn't speak English properly.

If measured success was worshiped in the world outside, then in the world inside it was vulgar. This may be dismissed as the prerogative of a privileged minority, who have now largely altered their ethos, but in America the medical profession could be said to be such a privileged minority, an intellectual elite whose accomplishments are of value to the whole community. The Bar Association might be said to be another, and it did not shrink from applying its standards to a former Vice-President.

It is not authority that is at stake in grading at all; it is the recognition of accomplishment, outside the restless hurly-burly of daily life and political action. Indeed, with science where it is today, it seems likely that our academic life will become increasingly hedged in with society's self-protective testings; already professors in our college, confronted with verbal illiteracy, are turning more and more to the *True or False?* type of examination. When you are able to blow up the human race, you become careful about the skills of those with fingers on the button.

At the end of an address on "Mass Education and Academic Standards" Irving Howe concluded, "I would rather we failed than lied." The words were no sooner out of his mouth than Manhattan Community College found itself at a loss to nominate a valedictorian for its graduating class since there were as many as fourteen Seniors with straight A averages. I submit that this is lying.

Buell Gallagher writes, "At the City College of New York, two or three junior members of the instructional staff became minor folk heroes overnight with their solution to the dilemma of giving grades that might lead to differential ranking of students: they gave everyone an A." I submit that doing so is lying. It was a case, all too common today, of teachers bribing students with good grades in order to get back good grades themselves. In 1974 as many as 46% of Yale's senior class graduated with honors. "They get a B and they bawl," said Eva Balogh, Dean of Yale's Morse College. Concerning the high proportion of A's at CCNY of late, Professor Irwin Stark of our English Department proudly proclaimed in May 1974, "last year seven out of my class of fifteen students achieved that normally elusive grade." Which, being interpreted, means: *he*, rather than *they*, had succeeded. Graduation from colleges like these is today accepted, as it is given, *cum grano salis*.

At CCNY today, some years subsequent to Gallagher's incumbency as President, the grade of F (Failed) has been abolished and WD (Withdrew) substituted for it. I submit that this is also lying. I continue to assign F's on my class rosters for those students who did not withdraw but failed, and with equal regularity the Registrar's office converts these marks to WD's. I read my equity, assigned me by the taxpayer, as to evaluate, not to mollycoddle.

By now the grading problem—by which the lack of grading is meant—has reached truly bizarre proportions, as the teacher reaches the end of the term, dodging spitballs and accusations of racism. One survey tells us that college grades have risen 10-12% in the past five years, while scholastic aptitude scores have fallen! Almost daily one hears of some preposterous new proposal to solve the problem, down to the final *reductio* of the student self-evaluation ("I'll save you the trouble," is my own answer to that one). Humanities teachers have so called into question their own identities by now that they truly deserve this nonsense. If they don't believe in themselves, why should students do so?

This difficulty does not assail Math. According to a survey of remedial Math students, taken at our college two years ago, over half the students confessed that they work harder in Math than in humanistic courses. It is perfectly true that I am behind some of my students in the content of written papers under focus—material from their chosen fields. I will read essays on the language of computers, of engineering, physics, calculus, which teach me more than I can empirically return. But this doesn't prove anything. My effectiveness must rest on other grounds. I am not ready to abrogate the authority of the subject to which I have first allegiance and in which I simply am more competent than they.

As presently operated, the university equity involves a kind of barter. By putting in time and money (though our students do not even have to pay) you expect the university to give you something of value. You expect a degree that denotes that you are thereby a superior person, now qualified for a better job than most in society. In exchange you agree to submit yourself to an evaluative process.

For somewhere along the line, in our society, there is going to have to be such. The ditchdigger (Construction Engineer) does not to date have to have a specialized degree. The higher salary and privilege that accompany the latter require earning. But let us assume that you give everyone a university degree. That still would not suffice. In order to earn money in a job, everyone—from a printer to a diamond cutter—is going to meet on the way some qualification of license; and those imposed by unions have been growing notoriously stiffer. Thus the liberal humanist, genially giving everyone an automatic A, is doing disservice to his students, as well as showing the greatest condescension of all.

There is perhaps another course. It stems from the view of optimists like Matthew Arnold and William Morris, who hoped that, before industrialism overcame us all, we might be able to make of every man a deeply imaginative, a whole, individual. Those who worked with their hands could become truly cultured. Arnold, in particular, made an effort, in the words of Northrop Frye, "to separate the ideal of leisure and cultivation from the members of the dominant class who embody it." In Arnold's day leisure was a class concept. By enlarging and educating it, you would break down classes.

Today this is different. We are back to another conception of the educational equity altogether; we are approaching leisured Virginia Woolf, who saw it as fruitless to "teach" anyone literature. At Oxbridge it was possible to get a degree, provided you "ate your dinners," without attending a single lecture. It was not possible to get one without passing an exam. Aye, there's the rub. Our society is somewhere, at some point, going to ask to see our credentials, even for Yoga, Zen ping-pong, or African basket weaving. To postpone the confrontation does not seem very helpful—except, as a teacher, for yourself. In short, by giving all A's you are shirking.

In the American city two elements operate on this question. First, there is the total permissiveness behind the community and city college experience. The emphasis on self-expression rather than self-control in the average city high school cripples any attempt to impose structure thereafter. Structure is an establishment Beelzebub. Seize the second. In doing so you may even win a Pulitzer Prize. Here is a San Francisco high school "Teach," Florence Lewis, describing a typical pre-college classroom situation today:

> In a class that had no walls, there romped a teacher, a happy colt; pony tail, glasses, sex undetermined really. Jocko by name, after the clown, not the strap, never Mr. Jocko. Jocko it was who greeted a still traditional group of five or six who came to register in his class early one day in late September. Refugees they were and rejects, from sitting in rows, systemwide grades, curriculum, homework, teacher, filet of sole. Colt and kids exchanged names. Second names "verboten." First names only. Second names too reminiscent of mothers and fathers. Hands touched in greeting. Very nice. Students sat on the tables or on the rugs or off the chairs. No desks. Not even for teacher.

It is obviously difficult to repair this situation. On a slightly more sophisticated level, it derives from the kind of "inquiry environment" encouraged by Paul Goodman, Edgar Friedenberg, Neil Postman, Charles Weingartner, Old Uncle Tom Cobley, and all. Here the teacher is deposed to buddy. In *Teaching As a Subversive Activity* the Postman/Weingartner team tells us that "the inquiry environment, like any other school environment, is a series of human encounters, the nature of which is largely determined by the 'teacher.' 'Teacher' is here placed in quotation marks to call attention to the fact that most of its conventional meanings are inimical to inquiry methods." These methods (owing considerably to Jerome Bruner's *The Process of Education*) turn out to be a mish-mash of parlor games and playlets called "interactions," or some other educational jargon, where you ask students "not to write in complete sentences, but to respond in three-, four- or five-word phrases" to such questions as "What does hair feel like? Anybody's hair. . . .Describe the texture of skin. Feel it."

We then lead off with the left foot into the tautology that, since you are not teaching but living out society at large, and since society is corrupt (Postman/Weingartner give barely a single instance of anything that could be construed as even faintly favorable to America), you can cheat too; you arrive at the nationwide industry of forged term papers. Yet, in the argument that students can cheat because society does, I have never found anyone eager to suport the contention that, in that case, the professor can cheat also, when grading. In a manner of speaking he does so already in the humanities; but he does not call it such.

Second, unlike science, art involves certain permanent values. In the constant revolutionizing of reality caused by science, it devolves on the arts to safeguard intellect, and stability. Our life has become too sensational of late for us to be able to be conscious without the filter, or fulcrum, of art. The repetitive "aheadof-ness" of the industrial artifact threatens this principle of being. With science forever altering the objects under our scrutiny, we need art to confer value on what it desires to apprehend. Wyndham Lewis went so far as to hope that we would make art the master of science, and relegate the scientist to the "valet" of the artist. In both *The Art of Being Ruled* and *Time and Western Man* Lewis alleged that science was popular: "Science stands for the theory of *collective* life, art for the doctrine of *individual* life." Science was manipulating mob passions under a shield of bogus anonymity, reducing us all to goggling children. Who are we, half a century later, to deny such charges as we sit, *bouches bées*, in front of the flickering Box? But C. P. Snow, rather than Wyndham Lewis, is the ideologue of our municipal universities.

In this sense our students are the most sluggish of animals. They want everything for nothing in the barter. Down with grades and grading. Guarantee everyone an automatic degree and a $25,000 job on graduation. The Deans applaud from the podium.

There are no two ways about it. Nobody wants to have to evaluate a fellow human being, but if your contract includes the signing of grade sheets, and it is in the interests of society to fulfill that contract, you should not shirk the task. Nor, in passing, can I see why grading on a bell curve is often derided as another example of deadly rote, since it protects the less gifted; it also in English, at any rate takes the teacher more, not less, time.

All academies would surely agree that the breakdown in grading standards began when, in the second half of the sixties, college was a shelter from the draft and you were supposed to be sending a kid to certain death in the paddy fields if you gave him a C. At this point the social contract seemed to have broken down. What was the point in fulfilling a compact with a society that was showering napalm on Asiatic peasantry?

It was around this time, too, that life within an urban college like ours began to deteriorate seriously—not only in the muggings and trashings, of which everyone had some story, but in the ubiquitous stealing that went on. No equipment could be left around for more than seconds unattended. Faculty carried key rings worthy of medieval jailers. Notices went up like confetti in the library and student lounges warning of the almost instant thefts everywhere for, as one lady professor mournfully remarked to me after losing her second pocketbook in a single term, "The students steal from each other all the time; I can hardly blame them for stealing from me." No new book of value lasted long in the library and one's office was emptied of any texts of any going value at Barnes and Noble. My own was, several times, and once a mugger came down through the plasterboard ceiling while I was sitting at my desk (he was so high on junk he scarcely knew where he was). You would be crazy to keep an encyclopedia where we work: in a single week of the fall 1975 semester a 16mm. projector and a piano were stolen from our new Leonard Davis Center, the latter while a class was in session. You also had, as an English composition teacher, to do the bulk of writing assignments in class, otherwise you would simply spend your time correcting plagiarisms. Here, for instance, is Mr. Alfie Martinez of our college announcing his woes in one of our student newspapers dated April 25, 1974:

> Last semester I took a research course in my major. Halfway before the term was over, the instructor told me that my completed research paper, the only requirement for the course, was a fantastic A paper. What a beautiful feeling to be in love with. However, the instructor, after seducing heavenly joys from me, with his dormant penis (figuratively speaking) raped me. He gave me a B.

Mr. Martinez then describes trying to maneuver a grade change and coming up against a secretary who told him he was several credits short for graduating: "Boy! Did she bring out the sadist in me! But she was too fat for sexual fantasies, so I fucked up the files on her desk by sensually knocking them off of it." Terrorism of the secretariat (most of ours being Black) was a common tactic in student insurrection; again, knocking files off a secretary's desk hardly requires much courage.

After such breakdowns repair was hard. In the field of evaluating the humanities the best way seemed to some to be to make standards less and less definitive. By now almost every possible method of evading or subverting our duty has been dreamed up and, indeed, discussed at great length and expense. One last "solution" might be mentioned. I first came across it at one of those large gatherings held under the auspices of the communications division of the National Council of Teachers of English (NCTE), which meet annually to thrash over what the Mock Turtle called Reeling and Writhing. This convention happened to be held in a hotel at New Orleans.

It must be said that these NCTE meetings are more heterogeneous in level, and locale of participants, than any of the kind I have attended. Wandering into one of these ballrooms, and wondering what balls could have taken place there, you are as likely to watch a spokesperson from Diablo Valley College as from Tuskegee Institute, from Le-Moyne-Owen College as from the South Dakota School of Mines, all pouring some coruscating oratory into a lamp in the evident belief it is a mike. This is the nitty-gritty of English teaching; no Ivy around at all, mostly high school, community college, some state universities, and the service academies. On the sidelines publishers jockey for the huge state or city adoptions, giving away literally thousands of dollars' worth of books free at the end of the operation. And if Mrs. Front Porch wants to know why Johnny can't read or write today, she could do worse than put an ear to the ground to hear the march toward mindlessness that organizations like NCTE, as well as MLA, have been taking of late.

The plurality of this particular meeting promised to be its pleasure. Where else could you come across a symposium made up from the ranks of Spachenkill Union Free School, the Miami-Dade Junior College South (who always send a strong contingent), and the U. S. Air Force Academy? There was genuine concern about every aspect of English teaching, from hiring to firing, from techniques of classroom management to how to cross disciplines and survive. Recently, more and more symposia have been devoted to the vanishing art, or act, of grading. At this meeting I found the usual "workshop" in "How Can We Incorporate Women's Studies into the Freshman-Sophomore Curriculum?", a discussion of Conrad's *The Secret Agent* as sexist (two Mss. in stern tandem here), the reiterated affirmation of students' rights ("Helping Students Evaluate Each Other's Papers"), and the like. Seriously interested as a linguist in some enlightenment about "Indian Ways of Communicating," I wandered into one emptyish hall where a Bella Abzug in a headband told us what slaves to mercantile culture we were. I strolled over to "What Grading Policies and Practices Should We Be Adopting?"

The answer was none. After all, if you regard a liberal education as does Edgar C. Friedenberg, as so much collaterally shared experience, you clearly need no testings at all. But in New Orleans I was introduced to what is called Contract Grading, which is something that has, under various guises, taken hold; our own P/F (Pass/Fail) grade, which a student can elect to take at the start of a term, and which almost invariably comes out with the former, is a minor mutant of the scheme and I am glad to say it is now being declined as a record of accomplishment by most major medical schools. In this system, since it is undemocratic as well as sexist and racist to grade, you *contract* with each student at the start of term for a grade, based on how many papers he or she wants to do. A Black student in the audience who asked what happens to one who wants a true grade was met with blank stares, and a pitying silence. Each term now I am beset by bellicose students who have received low grades in some exam and who ask, "Can't I make it up to a better grade by handing in an extra paper?"

This exchange is simply not the equity. I had not informed the thirty-four other members of the class that the terms of the test were that they could improve their marks by additional work. However, their anger at my refusal is more understandable than many of their angers, since their senior officials were playing the same game, giving "reexaminations" in the Biomedical Center of our college to (mostly Black) students in a calculus course and in a physical science course.

It transpired that these retestings were largely initiated by our President Marshak, their revelations jeopardizing the grant given to this center by alumni. The revelations were first made, before the *New York Times* and *Post* picked them up, in an issue of an undergraduate newspaper.

Eel-like, Marshak tried to twist out of the trap in which he had caught himself by euphemism. The "now, highly accelerated curriculum" placed "unrealistic" demands on students; therefore, "in order to make it possible for students to have additional preparation and instruction, opportunities for tutoring were provided, followed by retesting." He added, "This is a procedure followed in many academic institutions." It is not a procedure followed in any academic institutions and it nearly wasn't in ours when the Chairman of the Math Department refused to sign changes of grade in a calculus course for "retested" students, only to be overruled by a Dean.

It was perhaps the sheer gall in all this that turned our faculty's stomach, rather than its patent immorality. Here was a President "proving" that his program had succeeded by rigging the rules. As the campus paper that made the initial revelations editorialized: "The College seems to be waving two flags; one for academic excellence and the other for academic exceptions." Was it a coincidence that these exceptions were "minority" students? Wriggle as he might, Marshak could not get off the Morton's Fork of this dilemma. At one stroke he cut the ground from under the feet of those of us interpreting our assignment from the taxpayer as to sign a meaningful set of grades. "The President gives us a second chance," my sullen D's can now complain; "why can't you? You aren't by any chance racist, are you?"

Excellence with exceptions. The abdication is absolute. One cannot blame the young for spurning a system that demands so little of them. As Lionel Tiger and Robin Fox remind us in *The Imperial Animal*, "some of the difficulty universities throughout the world are having with the simple problem of discipline—let alone the more trying one of actually teaching and discovering—is that as a system of initiation, the university is far too arbitrary, unsatisfying, and undemanding for the young men concerned. No brave would count it a particular honor to triumph in history at Berkeley or Bombay. The challenge is somehow unmanly and the challengers themselves vaguely laughable and inept."

Yet a man like Marshak can always point a finger back at Washington. Affirmative-action programs in Berkeley have called for the wholesale abandonment of examinations, I.Q. tests, and other allegedly prejudiced measurings, one government proposal going so far as to require that felony convictions be ignored in applications for civil service employ. And this, of course, was under a government whose President, Vice-President, and other high officials resigned when accused of abuse of office, alongside Attorney-Generals and the like. Would a monarchy, one irreverently wonders, have done much worse?

But higher education is supposed to have a higher morality than gutter politics. The dishonesties of the former are the true insolence of office. For if you can reexamine ("give another chance to") students in the sciences, imagine how justifiably angry they wax toward anyone conferring low grades in the humanities. Irving Howe put it well when he said, "The only unforgivable sin toward students is condescension, and the worst form of that is to celebrate incapacity."

9
The Academic Supermarket

A year or so ago the English department in which I teach met in solemn deliberation. "The great Seraphic lords and Cherubim / In close recess and secret conclave sat." The errand of the exercise? How best to sell our courses to the students. Advertising posters, tub-thumping at registration, even commercials for Shakespeare Two over the college radio station were bruited.

Eventually a lot of this happened. A department that in my own career had swollen from thirty or so to, at its largest, some two hundred by virtue of compulsory remediation ("compensation") suddenly found itself in the absurd situation of having nothing to teach. They had said that the student was always right and here was the student yawning his head off at them. There were the required writing courses for reluctant Cubans, but otherwise we were addressing the ether.

At the start of one term I had been allotted a course in Modern British Poetry, beginning with Hopkins, Yeats, and Hardy, and four students out of a college of 25,000 enrolled for it; those four, incidentally, comprised the kind of minority within a minority that gets short shrift from a "liberal" college today.

The course was scrubbed; if it had been called Modern BLACK British Poetry, and only two mortals had opted for it, it would not have been, and I was assigned, within two days, the usual Basic Writing for immigrant Hondurans. After all, was not the revolutionary "poetess" Toni Cade (Bambara) now pontificating in our ranks and had she not, as one of our students, written the following criticism of our offerings in the leading student newspaper?

> A brief glance at the bulletin will reveal that the English Department is still dipping out of the old Anglo-Saxon bag, the snobbism and racism of which has its roots in the Jamestown Settlement and was nourished from generation to generation by Anglophiles like T.S. Eliot, for example, who were committed to the belief that the Anglo-Saxon tradition was superior to all.

And whose major work, if I am not mistaken, showed that tradition toppling into its grave, with fragments of Sanskrit and various Third World cultures envisaged as revivifying elements. But that's how wise they are these days. The only way venerable professors can now get students actually to take literature courses at our place is to put up jazzy posters, sit around the registration tables looking fashionably sloppy and hippy, and guarantee A's without attendance.

Several issues can be seen to have worked themselves out in this silly spectacle, for which, as usual, the taxpayer is footing the bill. In the larger social context truth has been so degraded that there seems no such value available in contemporary affairs. The basic social truth—justice—gets eroded all the time. In impossibly attempting to redress past injustices, we are creating, as Hegel warned us we would, further injustice; HEW, we shall see in the next section, proposes to redress victimization by victimizing others, about whom it appears, as a government agency, astonishingly callous.

But can the principle of justice stand up in the face of plea-bargaining as it exists in America today? In the case of the Clifford Irvings, the Swiss authorities remarked in this matter, "We are not merchants." When you can exchange a few years in jail for some vague form of "cooperation" with the authorities, the judge loses his role. Similarly, when forty million televiewers saw Sirhan Sirhan assassinate Robert Kennedy (or Jack Ruby kill Oswald) and were then compelled, by the laws of newspaper reportage, to call the assassin the "alleged" murderer (a new entity), a serious fracture of truth, indeed a dissociation of consciousness, has taken place. Imagine walking down the street with your mother, seeing her shot by a "perpetrator," and then having to refer to him on the morrow as the *alleged* assailant. Watergate taught us many similar lessons.

Even historical facts are under attrition in this manner. History is now called "aristocratic." New data may modify our view of the Hiroshima holocaust, but we know that it took place as much as we can say we know anything. Yet Gertrude Himmelfarb has amusingly testified that, in her field, there are no historical assertions for today's students, only so many "interps." Well, since literature is composed of even more interps, it rather naturally falls by the wayside. I now rarely see literature papers from students that seriously attempt to establish the validity of an intellectual position; they merely offer opinions, like a movie review, or else restate the plot. Their authors shrug or are aggrieved when they then hear what they do not want to hear, although, in fact, methodical and consecutive argument would be most useful to them in their evident quest to bust society to bits.

For there is a lovely sense of relief in smiling benignly back through your new beard at the student who calls Shakespeare a racist sexist sharecropping pig. Since there is no absolute truth available in literature, you are scarcely responsible for it as an academic discipline, or even indiscipline. The only truth you and your student agree to in an urban technocracy is the empirical or apodictic. It is impossible, even at our college, to shop around for swinging courses in Math or Chemistry as it is in literature. Hence, the pathetic spectacle of professors scrambling over each other to be popular proceeds amain; at our shop you will find courses on Chaucer or Milton listed, but seldom given (due to lack of registrants), while those on rock poetry or the occult or the latest going vogue (and they go fast) fill to repletion. The Board of Higher Education is happy when they fill.

A few terms ago a pleasant young professor put up the idea of a course on vampirism. He met a deal of Ninian derision, but his offering got listed and turned out to be the most highly attended, by far, of any course within our English Department (Chaucer, Spenser, Milton, Shelley not given, although the last two of these were ardent revolutionaries and one pro-regicide). Young teachers fell over themselves to get it. To beef up my own productivity average I insinuated into the catalogue a course on Libertine Literature. I may now change this to Kung Fu.

You cannot possibly call this an English Department. It is a remediation station, on the one hand, a welfare agency to make illiterates vocal, and, on the other, an entertainment center. This on the principle put forward by our ex-President Buell Gallagher that "In the Aristotelian sense [what Aristotelian sense?], enjoyment, not utility, is the measure of the value of a liberal education, both to the educated person and to society." Consulting college catalogues from around the country, one finds enjoyment of a course the trend, when utility is not at hand. Literature, together with music and art, is a mode of experience inimical to what a technocracy defines as truth. Therefore the easiest way out—and the best-known way to keep your college solvent—is to treat it all as Fun: show films, listen to tapes, gawk at TV, do anything rather than read. The criterion for a college course is whether it is enjoyable.

But entertainment is not an aesthetic value. Some of the most rewarding instruction of my youth was also some of the most boring (Tolkien at Oxford, an almost inaudible as well as deadly teacher). A child who has held himself to a daily dose of Latin gets into Math more quickly than one who has not. Learning subjunctive verbs by rote may not be so much Fun as *Gunsmoke* or *Dragnet,* but it has to be done if you want to master a language. In entertainment the relationship between oneself and one's interest is really quite contrary to the proper educational congruence. It was the late T.W. Adorno who suggested that we learn best under conditions of "alienation," namely, when we are asked to make the effort to modify internal compulsions on behalf of the external world.

If degree of interest were to be made a criterion of art, then we might have to say that John Donne or Vermeer enjoys a fad, having for centuries been of only minority interest. But the American multiversity is specializing fads, within the humanities. Professors wait on the sidelines, cap in hand, until the latest students decide what it is they want to study, what new subject they want to pick off the supermarket shelves.

This again works against knowledge, since the most myopic student soon sees that there are certain ground rules or conventions governing the sciences; he cannot study Physics without Math. But he can, and does, study James Joyce or Richard Wright without having read Shakespeare, Swift, Dickens. You can be an English major at our college and not have read anything in literature prior to the twentieth century—in which you read mainly non-English writers, in any case. Furthermore, there just does not exist a real body of knowledge to match each passing whim—vampirism, rock, drugs, magic. As Frederick A. Olafson puts it: "Unless the present generation has been favored with a very much higher proportion of geniuses than those in the past, the most likely result of permitting student 'inquiry' to define its own areas of study will be to encourage the illusion that the world is new every day and to subordinate the business of self-qualification to that of self-expression."

But still the restless changing of courses goes on. This intellectual giant and then that among the professoriat suddenly has the key to *what the students want* (it is a prominent feature of the urban liberal always to know what the masses really want, with the result that he gets upset when they only want junk on TV). Courses are dreamed up to meet each passing vogue. In our case, the true cant of the supermarket system was exposed when it was found that a number of courses were being duplicated. Assume that Art Three (Drawing from the Nude) was popular. All at once it was found that this was being taught in at least two divisions of the college, the Art Department and Black Studies. Why could not the Black Studies students learn how to draw in the Art Department, where the course properly belonged, and so save the taxpayer a professor (most of the models were Black, anyway)?

Elaborate Ramistic responses began to emerge to this question—Bio Two evidently wasn't quite the same in the Biology lab as it was when the frog was put out for dissection in Black Studies, in Huey Newton Hall. When it was demanded that Arabic be taught at our college, we were lucky in having Professor Abraham Halkin, a rabbi and one of the most competent Arabic scholars in the country, teaching in our Classical Languages department. He taught one course in elementary Arabic for no compensation, until it was repeatedly disrupted by the customary group of comically clad Black Muslims who asserted that "Only an Arab can teach Arabic."

Halkin was a Jew. Rather than waste time arguing with hooligans who couldn't even pronounce their own language properly, let alone Arabic, he left.

In the same way, after Puerto Rican pressure on our Spanish professors (that dialect being one of the most debased of a lovely tongue), the Chairwoman of the Department of Romance Languages asked one of her teachers to compile a glossary of Puerto Rican terms, notably those met with in New York City. He did so and was instantly jumped on by SDS elements, who asserted that the list was "nothing but a collection of vulgarisms with the sole intent of projecting images of racism, drug addiction, sexual perversity and lawlessness." The Puerto Rican Student Union invaded the professor's classroom and generally made his life on campus unbearable. Confronted with the issue, President Marshak did nothing; he talked about "the building of bridges in the academic community" at the Faculty Senate meeting debating the affair.

In conclusion, one sees that in all this chaos the sciences are relatively undisturbed. No one was shopping around for exotica when building up a backlog for a medical degree, though one vigilant eye did spot a course on Black Math in one college catalogue, and it was not a typo for Black Mass either; thus the "arts" or liberal offerings once more appeared as so many hesitant and apologetic ancillaries to a technical education.

What has been revealed to us in this instance is the lack of confidence of the liberal professor in his *métier*. Course credit has been given at one university for candlemaking, at another for staining glass; at yet another, Field Work in Marriage ("masturbation should not be allowed to get out of hand") has been offered, while further offerings include courses in pollution, square dancing, and peace studies.

In New York there is a body that calls itself a college and gives credit for your work in your job—by which token everyone should have a degree simply for going about the daily life of a metropolis. At Antioch College a girl demanded credit for her participation—rock-throwing—in a series of "revolutionary activities" aimed by a student group at demolishing the institution. It must be said that sometimes the new students and the new professors deserve each other.

Anxious for approval from insecure and politically sensitive administrators above them, one arts department after another in the public institution will offer its *smörgasbord* of pastimes in lieu of education, in order to be able to beam blithely back at critics from behind enrollment figures. Why, their courses are filled. So might they be, too, if you offered a diet of live sex shows.

McLuhan to the contrary, the fact that the world is watching TV does not mean that the world is right. Assigned to give courses on films, I found that students generally enjoyed these, especially when I selected on the basis of sex and gore—and when they stayed awake; but asked at the end of term to articulate what they had actually learned from all this viewing (which had cost the college plenty in rentals), they remained mute or vague or sullen, or all three at once. I continue to be assigned film courses. You can get much enjoyment learning nothing. Many at our college do.

"The loss of substance in the liberal arts," writes Ronald Berman, Chairman of the National Endowment for the Humanities, "is already having demoralizing effects. Teachers unsure of their allegiance are unsure of their professions and of themselves. Students are leaving the liberal arts in droves. At Yale, at Brandeis, at Wright State University (all representatives of different points on the spectrum of American education), undergraduates are rushing to vocational or professional studies." The majority of students simply do not want to be taught by other students. But if you put the student before the subject in your professional allegiance, you do the former a grave disservice at the expense of the latter, and you reach the sorry state of affairs of the huge municipal college where the present author teaches. Surely it might be better to cease the hypocrisy and follow the example of Ferris State College in Michigan by giving the students credit for something *really* useful—automobile repair.

Finally, you will be found out. Public confidence is waning fast in these large tax-supported institutions. The teacher is under contract to teach a subject and one can barely subsume vampirism, rock, and Frantz Fanon under the aegis of something called an English Department. Lacking humane intelligence and a genuine belief in culture, these new humanities professors will soon also be lacking jobs while their higher administrators build themselves ever more expensive homes and construct "superuniversities" such as CUNY's plush Graduate Center on 42nd Street in Manhattan.

The truth remains that a liberally educated person is a superior person, and the frantic espousing of ethnicity and phenomena like magic and rock can be read, on one level, as the liberal's attempt to reassure himself that he has not lost his egalitarianism by having become intellectual (he knows who Walt Frazier is), while in fact racial disharmony is as bad as ever it was before ethnic studies and open admissions started. Bertrand Russell remarked that the reason truth is not found more often is that people don't want to find it. Having destroyed his subject, the liberal professor has destroyed himself. Soon, like the Cheshire Cat, there will nothing be left of him but his smile.

Racecourses
of Academe

10
The Race for Racism

Racism begins early in the modern American city. This is tragic. The Book of Genesis makes no reference to race and the children of our schoolyards are equally blessedly ignorant of melanin skin content. When Oren Shalit was born in Israel some few years ago he was registered by his father as: Nationality—Jewish; Religion—None. The clerk in the Ministry of the Interior changed these entries to two blanks. According to rabbinic religious law (Halakah), no one can claim to be a Jew unless born of a Jewish mother or converted to the faith. Oren's mother was an atheist. Lieutenant Commander Benjamin Shalit of the Israeli Navy took his case to court and won a decision from the Israeli High Court of Justice allowing, in effect, a Jew to be a Jew if he says he is one.

The Shalit case revived that of the "wondering Jew," Oswald Rufeisen or Brother Daniel. Born in Poland, Rufeisen worked for his country's underground in the war and fled to a Catholic convent when betrayed (allegedly by another Jew). After the war he entered a Carmelite friary near Haifa and eventually petitioned the Israeli government for citizenship, under the Law of Return giving every Jew the right to migrate to Israel.

The Israeli High Court denied his claim. It did so by deciding that the Law of Return is secular and that a Jew is not simply classified as such by religion, race, or ethnic stock, but rather on the basis of a common historical experience, or *Zusammengehörigkeit* (similar to Bertrand Russell's "orchestration" theory). In the words of Judge Moshe Silberg, "we do not sever ourselves from the historic past and we do not deny the heritage of our forefathers." This symbolic bond, then, was to be considered the equivalence factor.* "Jew and Christian," pronounced Judge Silberg, "are two titles that cannot be combined into a common subject."

But of course they are—in plural America. So are Jew and skeptic, in such famous instances as Louis Brandeis and Albert Einstein. What, moreover, of the fanatical Neturai Karta sect, of the congregation of the Lubavitcher, who live in Jerusalem but fail to recognize Israel? In fact, in the case of Brother Daniel, Judge Silberg stated that the priest might well have been considered a Jew in rabbinical courts! In short, *society gets the classifications it wants.*

When I arrived in America, I was asked to put my race on the necessary immigration form; this was not a defining term I had been accustomed to in England, so I simply put British and hoped for the best. The immigration officer changed this to Caucasian, and I felt rather grand. But I wonder now if he would have been able to tell me how many races there are, or why people with red hair should not be considered a race (as in Conan Doyle's *The Red-Headed League*). After all, he would have known how many sexes there were. Do Slavic groups

---

*This factor is almost the only one **not** found as within the "characteristic features of religion," in the list prepared by Michigan Philosophy Professor William Alston to show that "when a cultural entity exhibits all these features to a marked degree, we have an ideally clear case of religion" (**Philosophy of Language**, p. 88).

(including Slovaks, Slovenes, Serbs, Czechs, and Croatians) constitute a race? If not, why not? Slavs have not, as yet, started a minority drive for fairer representation on university faculties, though they well might, as may women desirous of playing in the backfield of the Baltimore Colts. That labeling categories mean what we want them to mean was once and forever exemplified in a headline that appeared in the San Francisco *Nichi Bei Times*—"JAPANESE IN MOSCOW COMPLAIN, MISTAKEN FOR CHINESE, ABUSED."

When we invent a class we assume some *quidditas* of equivalence, a special presence making two or more entities similar. This not only forms a present function, but makes possible future acts. Furthermore, the classificatory technique is typically reflexive; we can collect classes into classes (shoes into pairs of shoes, for instance). The Navaho, who were not exactly famous for Fem Lib, evidently sorted everyone into a brace of basic typologies—witches and non-witches. Both classes could be collected under the category *human being*. But in practice, for the majority of Navaho, the classification *witch* subsumed that of human being, rather than vice versa.

In this way, as in many HEW discriminations today, the labeled category tended to include itself, and formed thereby a logical contradiction (e.g., a Chinese Jew), one that doubtless assisted in putting the tribe out of existence. The denial of vote to Southern Negroes, and the formal deceit used to implement that denial, lay in the same inconsistency haunting us in educational "affirmative action" today. To cry "Are Negroes citizens?" as a lever for opening the voting booths was laudable, but also a logical fallacy, since in America *voters* and *citizens* are self-containing classes. To recognize this helps one to identify the true nature of the prejudice at issue, of the mind that was summarily saying, "Are Negroes *human beings?*"

There was a time in the Southern States when Negro was used as cognate with White, or Yellow, or What-have-you. But to say that someone is a "black" man, or a "yellow" man, or a "red" man, is to muddle the category with the defining attributes of that category. Justifiably enough, much capital was made of this by Malcolm X. It will be interesting to see how much new nomenclature has helped, or hindered, Black aspiration. Arriving from Spain, *Negro* simply meant Black; will *Afro-American*, accompanied with pierced nostrils and other accessories, prove more positive in connotation in the face of the repudiation of Black Power by increasing numbers of African states? Etymologically, Africa carries more derogatory associations, deriving from *a fero*—"from a wild place" (Partridge). But, of course, derivation is not meaning. However, one has to know rather more about language than most politicians, White or Black, before indicting the English language as a carrier of racism.

Is the human being I see in front of me a singer, a lawyer, a Communist, a ball player, a Negro? At one time Paul Robeson would have fitted all these categories at the same time. They are all *minorities*. Bias pours in when the term is vague (what does a *singer* signify?). Thus society screens out, selects, which of Robeson's minority claims it *wants* to class as a minority. We shall see that this is what HEW is doing, in the face of the law of the land. "Where anti-Semitism fades," writes the French Jew Georges Friedmann, "Jewish specificity tends to disappear."

So, if you are that huge, unwieldy office called HEW, the US Department of Health, Education and Welfare, you play Humpty Dumpty. When Black students at Antioch College set up Blacks-only facilities, in a mirror image of that injustice we had finally, after years of toil, broken down, it was not called *segregation* by HEW. This and other similar actions (many challenged, some successfully, in the courts) were condoned by federal officials, who thus authorized exclusion of White students from all-Black dormitories and cafeterias on the basis of the Israeli High Court's *Zusammengehörigkeit* in the case of Brother Daniel. The Whites weren't being shut out because they were White, ran the argument, but because they did not have the historical background of Blackness. Furthermore, HEW likes to start our tots off early along this "track."

In most other countries education is administered under an autonomous ministry; to have it placed under or alongside other wide-ranging branches of governmental activity lends the agency, as we shall see, large and ominously indefinite powers. In 1974 there was issued an "Elementary School Questionnaire" that was to be given to fourth- and fifth-grade students (children of eight or nine)—or else. This question-naire encouraged the child to do what any kindergarten anywhere shows the child disinclined to do, namely identify himself or herself by skin color. The first question asked the pupils: "Which of these are you?. . .I am Black. . .I am White. . .I am Brown." The child had to tick off the relevant hue. Yellow or other shades (such as my own purple when first reading this document) were omitted.

These questions, all solemnly sponsored by Washington, grew ever more repulsive as little Johnny was encouraged to spy on his parents: "How do you think your parents feel about Black and White students going to the same school together?" Multiple-choice answers of Black, White and Brown were provided. Orwell's child "Thought Police" could have done no better as our youngster was then encouraged to sense out incipient racism in his *teacher*: "How do you think your teacher feels about Black and White students going to the same school together?. . . How do you think your principal feels about all different kinds of students going to the same school together?" And so on.

Of course, this is precisely what South Africa has been doing for so long. In 1966 Sandra Laing, a dark-skinned South African, was classed as *Cape Colored* (i.e., of mixed-race descent). In July 1967 she was reclassified as *White*. What we have all championed for so long, namely, recognition of the common human bond rather than identification of skin "differences," variegated as these can be (for instance, in the southern Caribbean), is brutally brushed aside by the federal juggernaut. An embattled Nixon probably barely knew what was going on in this department, and perhaps cared less.

But one would hope that college presidents might make more of a stand than they have to date against federal felony. Ours sent round a faculty questionnaire whose computer print-out directed us to check one of the following: "Black White Prt.Ric. Orient Am.Ind OtherSpan Ital.Am. Other—Specify." This was bad enough. The cognate of Puerto Rican is not Other Spanish but Venezuelan or Cuban or Mexican, many of which citizens might intensely dislike being classified as Spanish at all. But what was worse was that President Marshak accompanied the questionnaires with a note saying that if we failed to fill them in, they would be filled in for us, in any case.

This aroused a storm of protest, which was intensified as a similar set of these questionnaires was sent out to students; concerned community groups, even the New York Board of Rabbis, accused those administrating the program of being unconstitutional and illegal. Marshak replied that, in consonance with HEW's affirmative action goals, he was trying "to ensure greater opportunity in employment for minority groups and women." As *Women* had not been included as a category on the questionnaire, one assumed that

social-security data and given names would tell their tale. I
have had students in my classes whose first names might have
been of either sex. I should like to know what sex was assigned
by Dr. Marshak to my students whose first names were:
Aljean, Alyanak, Ceil, Czerny, Nayuin, Snydor, Tok? And if
he or his minions put down *Female* alongside Alison, Evelyn,
or Jocelyn, they could well have been wrong; those are men's
names in England, too.*

But the infliction of these adult distortions on very young
children is particularly unpleasant. For once, it is encouraging
to report that this governmental dictate was repudiated (partly
thanks to the fact that unions are tougher than college
presidents). The head of the New York City Board of
Education and the NYC Chancellor, urged on by several
courageous Black superintendents and teachers, refused to
allow the questionnaire in question to be distributed to their
pupils. HEW's answer? To refuse over $1 million in granted
funds to the impoverished children of New York's overcrowded District 19.

So you start them off early and, with luck, by graduate
school you will get the following result: "Dianne Howell, a
graduate student of psychology at the University of California
at Berkeley, likened her white classmates to 'the wallpaper.'
'They're there. They are just there,' she said" (*New York
Times*, April 4, 1972, p. 57).

These repellent polarizations, which I shall examine
more closely in the following pages, are doing real damage to
the American social fabric, one that depends as never before
on interracial cooperation. To its honor our union, the United

---

*The whole sick story of this questionnaire, and of Marshak's behavior in trying to
implement it, forms chapter 17, "Bias Disguised as Antidiscrimination" in Louis
Heller's **The Death of the American University**. At this time, too, we received a
directive signed by our college Ombudsman urging us, in true Hitlerian fashion, to
sniff out racism in our colleagues, though never, for some reason, in our students.

Federation of Teachers (AFL-CIO), recently refused to collaborate with a national TV network in supplying a spokesman for "the Jewish point of view" in education, in order to pit such, on the box, against "the Black point of view." We argued that such a confrontation, even if deemed dramatically desirable alongside old Perry Mason shorts, was educationally factitious and pernicious. There was no Jewish point of view about basic pedagogical principles any more than there was a Black or Beige point of view. There was education, and we wanted to get on with it. The network, needless to say, proceeded to choose someone of their own.

It is the same with Washington. When, in the face of the kind of absurdities of favoritism I shall instance below, HEW appointed its own Ombudsman, twenty-eight-year-old Samuel H. Solomon, he began to come up with considerable evidence of "reverse discrimination" or vastly preferential treatment for color groups of the then director's choosing. But, despite the splendid inscrutability of his communications, the wisdom of Solomon was soon repudiated by his seniors. Let us examine how our government defines a race by any other name.

11
I, Too, Am a Minority

Writing in *Commentary* (January 1972), Earl Raab put it unequivocally: "One of the marks of the free society is the ascendance of performance over ancestry—or, to put it more comprehensively, the ascendance of achieved status over ascribed status." Who can quarrel with this? The ideal was for long the glory of American academe. Any British transplant breathed a sigh of relief at the relative lack of social snobbery in the American university to which he came. Daniel Boorstin asks: "Is a Black caucus any more respectable than a White caucus?"

The answer given is the case of the shackled runner, an image widely used by HEW. In the hundred-yard dash one runner has had his legs socially impeded, as it were. The race must be run again with his shackles off. However, many now feel that today this runner has not only had his shackles taken off, he has been given an unfair ten-yard start. In fact, it is the other runners who are being handicapped on account of the presumed actions of their ancestors. As a Jewish engineering student shouted out on our rioting campus once, "I'm responsible for what I've done in this lifetime, not the last." To which one could add—"And he didn't do it anyway."

The theory of historical injustice proposed in this instance claims that since society imposed a wrong in the past, it must pay a penance now and compensate for that wrong today. This would be a little late for all those who were hanged, or judicially tortured, in past centuries and, as Raab rightly remarks, "there is no way to measure the exact relationship between ancestral wrong and current damage for any given individual." To see just how meanly the individual is being officially subordinated to a social integer by such bias, let us look at one such hundred-meter sprint.

In March 1971, the San Francisco School Board decided to eliminate or "deselect" seventy-one administrative positions in a servile bow to the new HEW guidelines. The sense of *guiding* will be seen to have been used rather loosely here. The Board used nine categories for what might be called the winning spot, in the following order: Negro/Black, Chinese, Japanese, Korean, American Indian, Filipino, Other Non-White, Spanish Speaking/Spanish Surname, and Other White.

One need not pause over the absurdities of these preferences—the allocation of only fifth place to one of our most disadvantaged groups, while the whitest of Other Whites can linger under Spanish surnames—nor enter into the assumption of the Board that these distributions represent equally "the racial and ethnic distribution of the total school population" as well as of the Bay area, in general. One is forced to echo Orwell, out of *Animal Farm*, that "all animals are equal but some animals are more equal than others."

Here is racial prejudice, naked and unashamed, in practice, and given the sanction of the U.S. Government. At a hearing in the San Francisco case, the following exchange took place between the attorney for those to be deselected and the School Superintendent's representative:

Att.: Do you know that Armenians, as well as being a minority ethnic group, have had a history of persecution and disadvantage?

Rep.: No, I never studied that.

Att.: Did you ever hear of the persecution of the Armenians by the Turks?

Rep.: Not as I recall.

Att.: Did you ever hear of the disadvantage which Armenians in California suffered in Fresno and Bakersfield?

Rep.: I am not aware of it.

Att.: If the respondent in this case says: "I am an Armenian and I want to be treated as a separate minority," what would you do with his case?

Rep.: For the purpose of this, I would judge him to be "white" and put him in "white" because there is no specific Armenian classification . . .

Att.: Would you consider that the Jewish people were an ethnic group?

Rep.: Yes.

Att.: Do you believe that there is a history of persecution and disadvantage which the Jewish people have had: ˙

Rep.: I have some remote knowledge of this.

Att.: Now suppose one of the respondents in this case came to you and said: I am a member of an ethnic minority, one of the Jewish people, and I believe that by reason of our historical disadvantage that we would like to be treated as a separate ethnic group, what would your reply be?

Rep.: That we have no category for you as a Jew.

By virtue of its unusually brazen racism, the San Francisco case was the subject of much comment, perhaps almost as much as that of deFunis versus the University of Washington later. A minority, it was seen, came to be what you said was a minority, and administrations simply became more and more cagey in covering up their destruction of the Constitution in this regard.* I remember talking with the learned counsel to one private university at this time; in veiled

*Why call it **reverse discrimination** when it is discrimination (at least in the now corrupted sense of that term)? **Reverse discrimination** has a defensive ring; such actions are racism **pur sang**.

terms he told me that the only way they had been able to stop HEW (from breaking the law, that is) was by unearthing a few facts with which to twist HEW's own arm.

An Associate Dean of the New York School of Medicine, for instance, covertly consulted five New York State Supreme Court Justices before coming up with possibly provocative selections. After these deliberations a ten-page memorandum went out to the Association of American Medical Colleges. It contained this clause:

> Establishing given percentages or quotas of minority students to be accepted in a class presents predictable problems. This should be avoided at all costs. It is possible to achieve the same results without giving the appearance of restricting portions of the class for designated groups.

The evasiveness speaks for itself.

None of these cases has so far succeeded in altering what might be called the local price of fish. In the spring of 1974, three years after the San Francisco case had been exposed in the press, and after the deFunis affair had toiled up to the Supreme Court, the CCNY Faculty Senate witnessed the following confrontation between its President and a Jewish faculty member troubled by the former's quota-like stipulation of an entering class of "minority group students" for his (largely Jewish-financed) Biomedical School:

> "What is a minority?"
> The question, of course, was directed to the committee that had framed the resolution. Yet Dr. Robert Marshak, the President of the college, rose to reply.
> "You know what a minority is."
> "I used to, but I'm not sure any more. I'd appreciate an explicit definition."
> Dr. Marshak shrugged and rolled his eyes in a gesture of exasperation. Clearly, he believed that I was being obstructionist —as usual.

"Blacks, Hispanics, and Chinese."

I hadn't expected such a forthright reply.

"What about Armenians, Greeks, Italians, and Jews—or other groups that used to be called minorities by a simple mathematical measure? You don't mean we are to exclude them from the category of *minority,* do you?"

"Yes."

"Then you mean we are going to have a quota system."

"It's *not* a quota system."

"If we admit or reject specific groups according to stipulated percentages, it's a quota system."

Dr. Marshak leaned on his cane—he was just recovering from a stroke—the muscles of his face tensing and his hands opening and closing convulsively.

"It's not my definition. It's the definition of HEW. It's not a quota system."

"I don't care whose definition it is. If it meets the criteria for a quota system, it's a quota system."

At such a point as this, all pretense at fairness has clearly gone. When meaning becomes a function of utility and the status of a category depends on what people do with it, then language burlesques itself. The formalized madness of dividing human primates into *Aryan* and *non-Aryan* is repeated. In the Second World War Krum Heller, German Ambassador to Mexico, hoped to seduce Mexicans to the Nazi cause by telling them they were really Nordics, having migrated south by way of the Bering Straits. A similarly unbelievable blanket inclusion of this nature was that of Protestantism in Jewishness, made by certain French reactionaries in the last century. Both Protestantism and Jewish aspiration being revolutionary, *"Qui dit Juif,"* declared Alphonse Toussenel a century ago, *"dit protestant."* Charles Maurras was to agree with this paroxysm-as-classification, one more variation on Karl Luger's "I myself decide who is a Jew."

A parallel test for the fallacies of self-suffocating classes crops up occasionally in religion. A Chinese Jew might be held to be more Jewish than a Jewish Jew, were the diacritica to be set up appropriately. As the Israeli High Court itself has more than once hinted—other courts, other findings. In *The Black Jews of Harlem* Howard Brotz argues that Black converts to Judaism are basically manifesting intraspecific revolt, that of separating from other Blacks. Throw atheism into the debate, and all the agreed dissimilars—chaplets and synagogues, censers of incense and broken glasses—have to give way. The self-consuming nature of a religious classification is shown up for what it is, the whole paraphernalia repudiated. At this point the tolerant authorities break down. You will not find officialdom conceding atheism as an answer to religious category on government forms; but if you are allowed to believe, you should be allowed to disbelieve. In fact, the Constitution so suggests.

Prejudice will thrive when the cognitive nature of the classification is low. Say *Arab* and forget that Lebanon's Christian community is as high as 48% and that of Syria 25%, to say nothing of the loathing of Iraqi for Syrians or of Syrian Baathists for Iraqi. Marshak's *Hispanics* would presumably include fascist White Spaniards and Portuguese. His is rather a frustrated reaction than a classification.

Orwell noted that Gandhi, now largely lauded as a racial liberator, "did not think of people in terms of race." E. M. Forster's Fielding, a teacher in India, "did not realize that 'white' has no more to do with a colour than 'God Save The King' with a god." At the end of *A Passage to India* Aziz and Fielding, Indian and Englishman, are enjoying a friendly discussion when "something racial intruded—not bitterly, but inevitably, like the colour of their skins." Forster's parenthesizing adverbs are all-important here—*not* bitterly, but inevitably. Skin color is an inevitable, one of several determinants, like sex and age, with which we are put into this vale of tears. When it fails as an ascriptive lever in the academy, as defining a minority, it is sometimes answered that Blacks, unlike Marshak's Hispanics, were forcibly imported into America. This criterion is supposed to be accepted *on the same level* of cognition as determinants like age or sex. In order to qualify, your ancestors have to have been slaves. We are back in Dickens's Office of Circumlocution, or Kafka's castle.

"It all comes down to syphilis in the end," bemoaned Huysmans's Des Esseintes, in the eighth chapter of *A Rebours*. For today's activist on campus it all comes down to slavery. This is the unanswerable answer, before which you are supposed to quail and grovel.

The truth is that most nations have been slaves at some time. The British were enslaved by the Romans and their Queen Boadicea is alleged to have taken her life after having been publicly flogged (the origin of *le vice anglais*, perhaps?). But I cannot say that I may extract much capital out of this fact when I go into an Italian restaurant today. Many British were certainly enslaved again when the Japanese made them build the Burma-Siam railroad. During World War Two my father was in a Japanese prisoner-of-war camp for three and a half years and assuredly endured slave conditions worse than the average American plantation of the last century (this was Changi Island).

For, yes, there are slaves and slaves. Large numbers of White English were imported into both America and Australia for slave-labor purposes. Much more recently a huge movement of White forced labor was made by Stalin for what is now called the White Sea Canal. Alexander Solzhenitsyn has likened this slavery to that which built the Egyptian pyramids in 2,500 B.C. The horrors of Nazi and Soviet White slavery in living memory are unparalleled anywhere, with their torture, terror, mass burnings alive, and staggeringly horrible mistreatment of women and children. Solzhenitsyn estimates that sixty-six million men, women, and children went to "extermination through labor" in the Gulag Archipelago. These nauseous blots on humanity have happened *now*. Even today the slave population of the Gulag Islands is said to exceed that of most European nations. Are, as a result, Russian refugees from this terror granted especial favors in American colleges? No. Why not? Because they were not forcibly imported into the country. This is the joker in the deck, and it is very wild.

In America the Simon Legree stereotype became embedded in slave historiography. There is no doubt but that such creatures existed. Then work by men like Myrdal, Stampp, and Elkins began to run beside, and correct, something of the *Mandingo* image. Kyle Onstott's book was tosh, but it became popular, on very little initial publicity from a small publishing house, since what he was saying is, in a sense, what both sides of the vexed question wish to believe. The White liberal really wants the "Massa" picture to remain intact because it enables him to blame slavery, a monstrous institution, for all the iniquities (and inequities) of society; and it puts him on the side of the underdog. He could be said to be an abolitionist *après le jour*.

When the two-volume Fogel/Engerman *Time on the Cross* came out in 1974, the academic liberal was appalled. This book suggested that in a majority of cases slavery wasn't all that bad; owners rarely exploited Black females, only the more idiotic broke up slave families, while many slaves were well cared for, if only for the sake of the economy of the plantation.

This book aroused extraordinary anger. It was, for the liberal, the unthinkable. CCNY's Kenneth Clark could only say, "Would the authors recommend a return to slavery?" From the University of Chicago Louis Gottschalk fumed, "My reaction was: even if it's true, I don't want to believe it." Any more, presumably, that he might want to believe that between

1967 and 1972 the number of Blacks enrolled in college doubled, while between 1960 and 1971 the percentage of Black professionals—doctors, lawyers, engineers—leaped by 128%; nor that within one generation Blacks increased their enrollments in White higher-education institutions by 110% and now enter college at a rate close to that of Whites; nor that between 1960 and 1967 non-White employment (over 90% Negro) rose more rapidly than in the country as a whole. For slavery is the pistol to put an end to every argument, the silencer. It is, indeed, unanswerable and it exonerates the liberal from having to think through his society. The next time a student calls you "Whitey," try calling him "Sambo" back, doing a soft-shoe shuffle, and singing a plantation song at him—and see who wins the war.

In fact, Asiatics have been forcibly imported into, and deported from, the United States until present times. The case of the nine tailors was dramatized by the ACLU because this was a sample of what was happening on a larger scale. In 1942 the U.S. State Department imported from Peru nine Japanese tailors, to be followed by other South American Japanese, in the hopes of exchanging them at the time for valuable Americans interned in countries then occupied by Japan.

Actually, the nine tailors remained in the United States, moving from one Nisei camp to another, and when their use as so much human barter expired after the war, so did the federal government's interest in them. They were told they were to be deported to Japan for having entered the country without proper papers. An ACLU lawyer in San Francisco won reclassification for them, Washington eventually consenting to their deportation to Peru. But by this time Peru refused to permit their reentry. Only in 1954, after more than a decade of litigation and humiliating camp life, were the men permitted to apply for residence in the United States.

Shortly before she died, that indefatigable fighter for human rights, Pearl Buck, found a group of some five hundred Chinese who had overstayed the terms of their admission into the United States, and who were being shipped —not back to China (who refused to take them), but to Holland. The basis of this crazy classification was that they had entered the country from Dutch ships, thus had to be removed on Dutch Ships, to Dutch territory (that is, prison), though none of them had been to Holland and had no desire to repair the omission. As Miss Buck pointed out, "The situation is analogous to a Chinese seaman on an American vessel which he deserts in another country. Would the United States at the request of that country agree to the deportation of such a Chinese seaman to the United States?" In truth, the ruse was so much modern slaving, or press-ganging, since the luckless five hundred were offered the alternative of an Amsterdam hoosegow or a galley on the Holland-America Line.

Just as Marshak's *Hispanics* is a Humpty Dumpty term, meaning what you say it means, so *Asiatic* and *Oriental* are bogus category devices; after having been smeared with the latter epithet, S. I. Hayakawa said, "Since Buddha, Confucius, General Tojo, Mao Tse-tung, Pandit Nehru, Syngman Rhee, and the proprietor of the Golden Pheasant Chop Suey House all have 'Oriental minds,' it is difficult to know whether to feel complimented or insulted." What of the Trinidadian Chinese who has never been to China, speaks only English, goes to Mass, plays cricket, but looks strongly "Asiatic"? How many of those, playing nose or eye-count classification games in our colleges today, know that Chinese is currently spoken as a native language by more people in the world than any other?

In passing, too, I have often wondered at HEW's official adulation of Chicanos. After all, this group was not forcibly imported into the USA. It could be said that America annexed Puerto Rico, but it did not annex Mexico. Today the latter country is thriving, and those who leave it to seek work elsewhere are responding to an indigenous condition.

Yet we read, "All of the California State Colleges have been requested to implement a program of active recruitment of qualified faculty of minority background, especially Negro and Mexican-American." Is America then to solve every second internal national problem by special privilege for such nationals—now from Bangladesh, now from Mozambique, now from Cyprus, now from Tibet? By this token, or any other, Vietnamese should figure high on the listings of minorities to whom America owes reparation, but at present writing they do not. One ends up realizing that for HEW a *minority* is a locally sizable and vociferous voting bloc. In fact, Seymour Lipset of Harvard reports discussing HEW's policies in this sphere with a "high member of the administration" in Washington, and being frankly informed that "those who were concerned about the imposition of quotas did not constitute a sizable constituency." Those suggesting that reverse discrimination was taking place were, he learned, "politically weak groups in terms of votes they can affect on the issue."

Bureaucracy is, by its nature, destined to defeat logic when it wants to pigeonhole individuals. Taxation, treasury, postal, customs, welfare, immigration, and other such "services" are more likely to be consistently inconsistent than otherwise in their attempts to docket us all. By now there are small libraries of legal cases illustrating the unsatisfactory nature of human labelings, as to whether an athlete is amateur or professional (shotputter Davis classed as a writer on the 1960 U. S. Olympic team, while the teenage Russian gymnast Olga Korbut went down as an Army officer), as to whether plasterers are really miners (when they dig up floors), or women men (as in Veterans benefits), or a heavyweight boxer from the Argentine who insisted on accompanying his national anthem on a guitar in the ring at Madison Square Garden a musician or an unincorporated charity, and as to whether, when the San Francisco Police Department Bagpipe Bands wanted to perform publicly, the cops were really warriors since, according to the nearest Musicians Union, the bagpipe was an instrument of war.*

In 1967 the Association of Assistant Mistresses met in London to decide, among other things, whether they still wanted to be called *mistresses*. They voted not to change the term, even though some of the mistresses might have been mistresses. In certain parts of America a pregnant woman cannot collect unemployment insurance benefits because to do so she has to be able to work. It would then seem that such a woman could logically pick up unemployment disability insurance. But she is told that to be *pregnant* is not to be *disabled*, although officialdom has just informed her that that is what she is. Here, courts have in effect stated that a woman who is *not able* is not a woman who is *disabled*. Gogol was very good at this sort of thing. Kafka would have felt at home in HEW.

You classify human beings as you want to classify them, if you are a government official. In 1966 a Wisconsin woman learned that she had been Irish most of her life. In 1919 she had married an Irish alien living in the United States and, under a law in effect from 1907 to 1922, any American woman married to a foreigner took on her husband's nationality. The good lady divorced, and supposed her citizenship restored when the law was repealed. But the State Department saw otherwise. *Citizen* and *voter*, as remarked, may be cognate

*As Herb Caen put it in the **San Francisco Chronicle**, "Has there ever been any doubt?"

classes, yet this Irishwoman had voted continuously in America since 1922, because local election officials also assumed her status to be what she herself imagined it to be. Finally, you can take someone out of the human race altogether, if that should suit your purposes; the defense attorney for a famous sexual felon in Boston in 1967 claimed that his client was not a human being at all but "a completely uncontrollable vegetable."

Once again, fiat classes reflect us to ourselves. The hope is that, in academe at least, we are not living out a running Gogol satire. Unfortunately, these days we all too often are. When language is used as laxly as it is by federal officials, who then enforce ferociously, you have the lawyer's classic nightmare—semantic uncertainty coupled with rigor of correction—and can pour almost any ingredient that you wish into the well of the bias modifier.

This has become tragically clear in our colleges, which should be bastions of opposition to all these verbal bubbles blown out, with such messianic certainty, from Washington. Quite ludicrous, indeed psychologically fascinating, examples of intellectual injustice now not only obtain in this field, but crowd in on it daily. You savvy disfela man? He is what I say he is. I myself decide who is a Jew.

The Civil Rights Act of 1964 specifically prohibits preferential treatments in no uncertain terms. As head of HEW, J. Stanley Pottinger subscribed to this Act, in particular to Public Law 88-352, Title VII, Equal Employment Opportunity, Section 703, j (a passage of legislation well worth rereading today). Yet anomalies of caricatural proportions abound in the hiring of college personnel. SUNY sends to Brandeis and other similar institutions the posting of a vacancy in Judaic Studies; this department, we read, is "searching for a Biblical scholar who is either female or a member of a minority group (Black, American Indian.

Spanish-Surnamed or Oriental-American)." This for the Chair of a Judaic Studies Department. While the Arabic specialist, Rabbi Abraham Halkin, was stopped from teaching Arabic because he was a Jew, a university asks for an Indian or an Oriental to lead its Judaic Studies. Are we standing on our heads or our heels? Yet in our next section we shall see many other equally crass formulations. "There is," James Buckley remarked on the floor of the Senate, "a kind of marvelous absurdity about it all, as if Lewis Carroll and Laurel and Hardy had been called upon as consultants in the formulation of policy."

For, though everyone is acting as though he knew what a minority is, no one in fact does, because a minority is what you say it is. The term is not used in Executive Order 11246 nor in the 1964 Civil Rights Act. What Senator Buckley's office discovered was truly an Alice-in-Wonderland world of semantic evasion. HEW was confidently issuing, through its Office for Civil Rights (OCR), the following definition as part of its "Higher Education Guidelines": "Minorities are defined by the Department of Labor as *Negroes, Spanish-surnamed, American Indians, and Orientals. . . .*" This definition was said by OCR to derive from a Department of Labor document called "Revised Order No. 4" which uses *minority* or some form of the term no less than sixty-five times but *refrains from defining it once.*

Moreover, this Order dealt with a specific industry—the building industry—and to transfer its terminology to the university has been the fount of the trouble. To try to make boxing, where Blacks predominate, or opera, where Italians do, more ethnically representative would be met with hoots of derision. But OCR turned the university into "the contractor," under constant scrutiny from government reviewers.

The passages of the Order dealing with "underutilization of women" become baffling when taken out of the context of construction companies; of course there is a minority of lady bricklayers, particularly of those willing to strip to the waist in summer. A factor in determining whether you are employing enough women is "the size of the female unemployment force in the labor area surrounding the facility." Here there would clearly be considerable differences when teaching, or brick-laying, at Dartmouth or in Detroit, at Sweetbriar or in St. Louis. Senator Buckley found his first close definition of *minority* in an Appendix to a memorandum by Arthur A. Fletcher, then Assistant Secretary of Labor for Wage and Labor Standards, dated June 27, 1969:

> For the purpose of this Notice, the term minority means Negro, Oriental, American Indian and Spanish-Surnamed American. Spanish-Surnamed American includes all persons of Mexican, Puerto Rican, Cuban or Spanish origin or ancestry.*

Once this Pandora's box was opened, of course, academe was in for it. The Red Queen of HEW ran amok, shrieking for executions. Everyone took a large dose of Daniel Boorstin's Homeopathic Social Science (=the hair, or tuft, of the dog that bit you) and, in simple self-defense, declared himself or herself a minority. The principle was that, just as when everyone was a criminal, including possibly the President, the

---

*Compare a similar example of the tergiversations of officialese, in which the words themselves have power over the dice, this time from England:

For the purposes of this Part of this Schedule a person over pensionable age, not being an insured person, shall be treated as an employed person if he would be an insured person were he under pensionable age and would be an employed person were he an insured person. (British National Insurance Act, 1964, 1st Schedule, Part II.)

Vice-President, and sometime Attorney-General, then no one was, so you abolished racism by making everyone racist, as in the elementary school questionnaire instanced above.

Boorstin's Professor X. observed, correctly, that "'racism' was an evil only when it was not *universal*. By inoculating each section of the society with the special brand of racism appropriate to it, we can hope to give a virile new vigor to all American life." In this movement the Ku Klux Klan and the Black Muslims and the Black Panthers alike are pioneers. If this is dismissed as so much mischievous satire, what of the reality? Leonard Kriegel of our college writes: "Every few years we've simply traded in one victim for another. We could wash down the radical psyche as we washed away the stain of color. No doubt, given the rules of the game, radicals could trade in Blacks for Indians or Chicanos in a few years' time."

But what were the rules of the game? And after all, why not? If you put side by side HEW's "Higher Education Guidelines" and the Department of Labor's "Guidelines on Discrimination Because of Religion or National Origin," *issued in the same year,* you come up with the Government of the United States saying, in Senator Buckley's words, "that while members of European minority groups and certain religions are definitely victims of discrimination in business employment, it has also decreed, through HEW's Office of Civil Rights, that when it comes to employment on a campus, they are not entitled to the same regulatory protection that is now accorded to Negroes, the Spanish-surnamed, American Indians and Orientals."*

Boorstin's Professor X. sponsored a sociology of the absurd. Unfortunately this has been surpassed on our urban

*The European minorities protected by the Department of Labor guidelines were "Jews, Catholics, Italians, Greeks and Slavic groups."

campuses today, as the race for racism is on and everyone tries to find some cubbyhole of minority status from which to require preferential treatment. At our own college the ethnic and sexual splinter groups multiply so rapidly each semester, as the administration strives to quiet the chorus, that our leading student newspaper, *The Campus*, observed:

> The limitations and safeguards President Marshak claims he has established to avoid an inane proliferation of ethnic departments are grossly inadequate. The decision to limit future departments to groups comprising 5% of the student body or more is unworkable. Would a Jewish student whose mother comes from Lithuania and father from Germany be classified as a Russian, Lithuanian, German Jew or combination thereof? Where, since it is illegal to force a student to reveal his racial or ethnic backgrounds, would accurate statistics be required? It is quite possible that the specter of "an Italian Department, a woman's department and a department of sexual tastes," facetiously raised by one speaker, may come to haunt the faculty.

It is not only possible; it has happened already. Every variety of deviance must now be allowed its status as "minority." Our Professor Byrne Fone teaches a tax-funded Gay Literature course. It is parenthetically interesting that even HEW still pontificates about "women *and* minorities" (italics added) for of course the former form a majority they wish to have treated as the latter. Gay faculty groups are now coming out *à gogo* ("Take your hands off me, you heterosexual pig" is heard in the faculty cafeteria) and considerably embarrassing at least our own administration. It was Sade who wrote that the fact that nine-tenths of the world found the rose's scent sweet was no principle by which to oppress those who thought it loathsome.

By now I have seen an article, in New York's *Village Voice*, arguing for "liberation" for sadomasochists, and another on behalf of the left-handed ("Down with Righty!")

against whom manufacturers of kitchenware and golfclubs are biased. More recently still, there has been an amputee lib movement and also an adoptee lib drive—this to "liberate" adopted children to know their parents. But perhaps the most bizarre has been the Mental Patients Liberation Project (Mad Lib), another reaction to misclassification, with its own publication ("All the Fits That's News to Print"); the irony here is that such persons would sometimes prefer to be recognized, and tried, as criminals rather than be incarcerated incommunicado in a state mental hospital for a lifetime.

When still head of HEW, Pottinger was assailed, at Boalt Hall Law School, by militant women for favoring males, at Hayward State College shortly thereafter by Chicanos for giving preference to Blacks, and by the latter for preferring almost everyone else everywhere. No wonder he left. "And so," Senator Buckley summarizes, "our colleges and universities will find themselves forced to punch into their computer cards more and more categories of human beings so that they may achieve the exact mix of sex, race, religion and national origin that will be required to satisfy their ever more fastidious inquisitors."

In his Pulitzer Prize-winning *Democracy and Its Discontents*, Daniel Boorstin discussed with some dismay this Balkanizing of America. In one chapter, a lecture delivered at the University of Michigan, he addressed himself to "self-liquidating ideals," another version of his Professor X.'s Homeopathic Social Science and an apparent elaboration of Orwell's *1984* where we had read that "The very word 'war,' therefore, has become misleading. It would probably be more accurate to say that by becoming continuous war has ceased to exist." Boorstin defines a self-liquidating ideal as "an ideal which is dissolved in the very act of fulfillment."

Thus college presidents hope to dissolve racism by letting it be continuous and continually fulfill itself. They fail to see, or acknowledge, that organizing people into categories, or little competing collectives, is subversive of our system of government, which has always tried to defend the individual from the wholesale power of the collective unit; now it pays to belong to the latter. It is also subversive of society in a wider sense.

Ethnographers and anthropologists have long instanced the dangers to society of subcultures that cut themselves off from the main body on the basis of some minority pattern, which they then defend with violent aggression. Erik Erikson calls these "pseudo-species." They are artificial splinterings that should not be confused with healthy cultural variety; their prime aim is to attack the parent body. In New Guinea several hundred dialects are spoken, and championed, so that the operation of the society is impeded. Irenäus Eibl-Eibesfeldt writes, in *Love and Hate*, that

> there is danger in this tendency of groups to fence themselves off, for it is often done in a spirit of hostility. This is even true of the setting up of groups within ethnic groups. The tendency toward "cultural speciation" (sometimes known as "club-formation") mitigates [sic] against a wider social cohesion. What must be done through education for tolerance is to eliminate the element of hostility from man's habit of fencing himself off.

In the light of the present survey Irving Howe's comment then takes on a peculiar relevance—"it would be a dreadful form of intellectual condescension—and social cheating as well—if, in the name of autonomy of subcultures, we were to dissuade their members from trying to establish deep connections with the culture in which they are going to live."

This is tragically true. It has doubtless by now maimed one generation of minority students, to proceed in the reverse direction. For to tell a young and ambitious Black who struggles for a place in a college that its School of Engineering represents *White middle-class values*, and inveigle him into

African basket weaving or Soul Music, is deliberately to deprive him of those skills he needs in order to master Whitey's world, to say nothing of putting up bridges that will stay up, and be paid for.

Today, then, college kids can be disadvantaged for not being disadvantaged. We hear increasingly from the sons and daughters of poverty-level WASPS discriminated against though of minority status. We have come to learn of a new form of "passing." Employers (even "contractors") are prohibited from collecting data on their employees' race, religion, or national origin. When in June 1972 Mr. Pottinger warned CUNY that it had to provide such data (including sex) on its faculty or else lose $13 million in government contracts, he was told that the university simply did not have such listings in its personnel records, and that they were illegal anyway.

Pottinger pressed on, however, and CUNY attempted the census mentioned, which both students and faculty declined. It was extremely clumsily handled at City College. However, Pottinger's threat made its mark. Just as at the University of Michigan, into which he had also brashly sailed, some form of compliance to the letter of the HEW dictate had to be thought up, in order to provide such data without being conspicuously unconstitutional. Michigan dreamed up a procedure known as "self-designation," by which a staff member who was a Polish-born Brazilian-naturalized Catholic might enter his category as Black Muslim Female.

CUNY was cleverer, or more Machiavellian, if you prefer. It evolved a system of what it called "visual identification" of candidates for position. A memorandum went out: "The affirmative-action inventory is to be done by a *visual* survey [italics in original]. There *should not be a notation of any kind* as to ethnic background in either personnel records or permanent files. . . .Identification of Italian Americans will be done visually and by name. . . .Please remember, however, that each individual is to be listed in only one ethnic group." Visual identification was, of course, the method of Hitler's famous Mayor of Vienna.

It is no exaggeration to say that by now academic-preferment "passing" has reached the proportions of high comedy, reversing Blake's poem to the tune of "And I am Other White / But O! my soul is Black." Young assistant professors discover lost Serbo-Croatian aunts, ghost Magyar grandmothers, Croat stepfathers, Latin-American ("Hispanic") half-sisters. The AID (Americans of Italian Descent) bumper stickers increase in faculty parking lots.

Others transsexualize themselves expertly. Some change their names. I find myself clinging with more and more affection to the memory of my Malayan foster mother. In a leading scientific weekly there lately appeared advertisements for scholarly employ from a "Female Planetologist," a "Minority Group Ph.D," a "Physiological Psychologist, Ph.D., Chicano." In short, Ph.D., Chicano is a sounder qualification than Ph.D., Chicago. The candidate comes to understand that he or she is being hired for sex or skin color, rather than for any intrinsic ability. Surely the final condescension.

Paul Seabury has put a finger on this absurd "passing" by comparing it with the caste system in India. The comparison is by no means far-fetched. In British India preferential treatment was accorded certain castes, for obvious purposes. Gandhi actually opposed the plea of the Untouchables to be so favored, arguing that they would be better off assimilated into the main stream of society and that the establishment of more and more splinter factions would only damage India. It did. On independence the new government scheduled certain "backward classes" (cf. our "disadvantaged," "underprivileged," etc.) for favored treatment in official positions, notably the teaching profession, with the result that considerable pressure was created to be officially registered as "backward"—so much so that a 1964 Mysore Commission declared every caste but two as such and, Seabury tells us, "In Kanpur, recently, the son of a wealthy Jat family applied for admission to the Indian Institute of Technology and was rejected on objective criteria; he then reapplied as a member of an ethnically scheduled caste, and on this basis was admitted."

In concluding this dismal record, one is reluctantly compelled into a certain philistine satisfaction. Our great and all-knowing liberal intelligentsia, the darlings of the *New York Times Review of Books*, cheering on the disruptors and activists, were apparently powerless to perceive just what was happening to themselves. Staunch supporters of bureaucratic harassment when directed against their enemies, the "reactionaries" (like most of the best writers in English of this century, Yeats, Lawrence, Eliot), these zealots of the academy and of publisher's row are now getting a taste of the same, all in the name of justice and equality, right in the teeth. Upon which unedifying spectacle it is comforting to go back to the mouths of those babes and sucklings for whom the "Elementary School Questionnaire" was designed. A young teacher writes,

In teaching eighth-grade American history, I find it not only necessary but greatly enlightening to include lessons on the contributions of minorities to our heritage. After an excellent film on the American Revolution, one white student remarked that the film's narrator had continually used the term "Negro." He thought that today the preferred term would be "black" or "Afro-American."

Not knowing the answer, I posed the question to a student of African descent. "Sharon," I asked, "won't you tell us—what do *you* prefer to be called?"

Her answer had the simplicity of a child, but a wisdom far beyond her years. "Sharon," she replied.

12
Affirmative Apartheid

As delineated above, the Civil Rights Act of 1964 was concerned to spread equality of opportunity and, in so doing, to control "contractors," those bodies contracting with the U. S. Government and possibly guilty of discriminatory hiring procedures. Such behavior would, it declared under Title VII of the Act, result in the termination of such contracts. Even at the initiation of these procedures, voices were raised that such implementation of the Act might, in fact, result in a reversal of its stated aims.

In the universities implementation began to go forward on the basis of President Johnson's Executive Order No. 11375 of 1967, in which "The contractor will take affirmative action to ensure that employees are treated during employment, without regard to their race, color, religion, sex, or national origin." (President Kennedy apparently coined the term *affirmative action* in 1961, while none other than General Eisenhower had warned against what he dubbed the *military-industrial complex* earlier.)

Johnson passed away but his Order didn't. It became the dynamic of HEW enforcement procedures against universities that, when it was first given out, cannot seriously have been taken into account as federal "contractors," possessed of labor/management relationships. Nor, intentions being what they were at the time, was it probably imagined how, in this area of education, implementation would run over a lot of innocents, notably White males like Marco deFunis Jr., denied admission to the University of Washington Law School in favor of less-qualified applicants, and others like him who would have to spend money taking their cases to the courts (the Superior Court of the State of Washington found for deFunis, a Jew, as victim of preferential treatment of other groups). Nor did this apartheid stop at the universities: Edward N. Costikyan was denied his position as delegate to the Democratic National Convention since he was an Armenian-Swiss Unitarian; "if we non-young, male, non-Black, Armenian-Swiss Unitarians," he wrote in *New York Magazine*, "want to participate, I guess we'll have to organize, too." Surely his was a minority, if ever there was one.

Finally, it seems not to have been anticipated that, in the field of higher education at any rate, affirmative action would turn into a new version of Jim Crow separatism, translating equality of opportunity into numerical equivalence, until you would have the spectacle of the Superintendent of Schools in San Francisco revealing a plan to hire no more than 20% of Other Whites for administrative positions in the first year, no more than 10% in the second, and none at all thereafter until ethnic proportions of his administrators matched those of the school population. Northwestern subscribed to faculty appointments "at a rate of 25% women and racial minorities," with SUNY at Albany coming up with "a policy of one-to-one hiring of minorities affecting all the administrative staff." The Chancellor of the City Colleges of Chicago announced in 1974 that "when 52 systemwide contracts expire in July for teachers, many qualified whites will not be rehired and blacks will be sought to fill their jobs." Harvard was warned not to "raid" Black college faculties. "The Provost of Stanford," we read, "has asked our Department to make a special effort to assemble a roster of Chicanos."

Doubtless this was due to a difference, one that grew alarmingly, between what the Executive Order said and what HEW ordered. For instance, Sacramento State College took the general rather than the school population as yardstick of proportionate employment, declaring itself determined "to recruit, hire and promote ethnic and women candidates until they comprise the same proportion of the faculty as they do of the general population." Brown University interpreted the "good faith" measure handed down by HEW as the proportion of *"available members of such groups in the labor forces."*

At first OCR appeared to accept this labor-force interpretation; it sounded good; but then the agency looked around some sensitive corners and changed its mind (obviously, you might not find enough women employed along the feed-belts of, say, Seattle). Finally, when courageous President Spenser of Davidson College persisted in a lengthy correspondence challenging HEW's regulatory authority altogether, he was left alone. A conscientious address by Robert F. Sasseen, Dean of the Faculty at California State University, San Jose, concluded that a completely new concept of rights was being introduced by HEW's actions, one substituting proportional result for equal treatment and opportunity:

Let us suppose that the Executive Order means what HEW says it does. Does this make a difference? In all candor, I believe that it makes a momentous difference. In that case, we are confronted with a constitutional crisis potentially as serious as any this nation has seen. If this purely executive order commands proportionate employment in the name of equal treatment or equal opportunity, then the President of the United States has assumed a prerogative power beyond all limitation, contrary to the Constitution, and in substance utterly subversive of the principle of equality which is the foundation of all our law and all our morality.

How did it happen? Federal "contract" funding in American education today is massive, almost all-inclusive. According to the 1970 Report of the U. S. Commission on Civil Rights, the federal government is in fact the largest employer in the country. The so-called "Great Society" Congresses (88-89th) passed twenty-four major legislations increasing the federal authority in American education. Our government now provides 20% of all monies expended on elementary and secondary schools.

Throughout the U. S., school districts live or die by Emergency School Assistance Act grants, and you won't get one unless you collaborate with the new racists in Washington, all saying that they are fighting racism. Title One spent some nine billion to assist education in ghetto areas.

Even so, the nature of federal financing of colleges was probably little known until the HEW bulldozer got going. By the mid-sixties most major universities were 30-60% dependent on federal funds. The University of Michigan, for instance, when HEW first hit it, was due to lose as much as $60 million a year if it failed to act "affirmatively" within thirty days. Despite local affiliations, systems like those of CUNY and New Mexico State were found to be far more heavily mortgaged to the federal government than was generally realized. Several colleges that considered themselves private were brought up short, President McGill of Columbia being forced to say at this time, "We are no longer in all respects an independent private university." More recently, the Carnegie Commission has called on our government to increase its college funding to $13 billion by 1978. In short, just as no one was quite ready for physical assault on the universities in the sixties, so few anticipated the actual clout HEW would carry when it started to implement the Johnson Order in upper education. This was no social reparation; it was naked revenge.

Such became clear when HEW's Office for Civil Rights threatened to cut off $30 million in federal funds for Columbia University, which had not been found guilty of any discriminatory practices at all. On the contrary, it had made painstaking efforts, through sundry committees and thousands of dollars, to evolve a program that would satisfy the then head of HEW, J. Stanley Pottinger, who did not mind openly boasting, "We have a whale of a lot of power and we are prepared to use it if necessary."

Clearly it was impossible for Columbia to fire tenured members of its staff simply because they were suddenly found to have certain group characteristics which, in any event, it was illegal for the university to endeavor to discern. Columbia was being required to break the law, at the pistol point of confiscation of funds, by a government office. Since it could not satisfy all masters, and was not allowed to cull the ethnic, sexual, or religious data of applicants, it tried to wriggle free of the tightening straitjacket by asking applicants for tenured position to bring forward a letter of recommendation from some "minority" scholar. This last element was in short supply. In 1972 there were only 1,500 Black Ph.D.'s in the whole country, one study claiming that less than one percent of all Ph.D.'s granted has gone to Blacks. Lowering your qualifications in order to force Blacks into tenured positions was, apart from anything else, rather unfair to those (including minority members) who had been told that such a degree was an essential and had sweated to get it.

The ironies began to abound as HEW cast its net around; from 1970 to 1972 over 350 colleges were charged, for instance, with discriminating against women (why not all of them?). As these ironies began to be exposed, it was seen that OCR, once supported by radicals as championing the individual, now sought similar acclaim for judging by group. But less attention was given to the basic tenure problem, although never was the self-destructive psychology of the academic liberal better revealed than in the movement to which many teachers lent their pens and voices in order to abolish tenure. Here, surely, was another death-wish or attack-anything phenomenon. Nat Hentoff wrote a stirring article in *Village Voice* on how outmoded and unneeded teacher tenure was. It has never been more needed, of course, nor incidentally more useful to the genuine liberal.

In most states academic tenure followed similarly protective civil-service laws, which came into being to safeguard public employees from being politically victimized. I can vouch that in my own department it is only the tenured who dare speak up and, indeed, we decline from asking nontenured personnel to put their names to petitions or advertisements critical of the administration, which would involve them in reprisals. A parietal part of tenure is peer evaluation, common to the legal and medical professions, and the attack made on it in the late sixties by those sheltering under it was mind-boggling. Why not go out and shoot yourself? Some did.

That tenure protects incompetence is certainly the strongest, in fact only single serious, argument against it. But we now have, in any case, governmental sponsorship of such incompetence when HEW issues a directive on criteria such as the following: "Neither minority nor female employees should be required to possess higher qualifications than those of the lowest qualified incumbent." Here is HEW taking as its norm the accidentally institutionalized village idiot in our ranks and openly turning its back on any true standards of qualification. Try this directive on the bricklaying trade.

Moreover, mediocre minds tend to pick other mediocre minds to teach beside their own; anyone who might rock the boat is avoided. A decade or more ago the Middle States Association evaluated the college at which I teach and found, for its principal criticism, academic inbreeding. We were clearly appointing too many of our own graduates. Loud were the voices declaiming against this opinion. We had, they said, picked the best candidates available, regardless of college of origin. Our own simply happened to have sent up a lot. The same voices now shout out the reverse, that we should select by origin rather than ability.

For tenure is given only after a probationary period of peer evaluation. If you have evaluated poorly for five years, that is your fault, and yours the burden to bear. This error factor is the price we have to pay for the freedom of tenure. Would you prefer to have your teachers evaluated by the nearest steam fitter or soda jerk? And life can be made tolerably miserable for an incompetent or lazy teacher.

Finally, tenure is by no means irrevocable. In most states tenure exists for as long as there is a job for which to have tenure. If the enrollments of publicly financed students so shrink that teachers are in surplus, the public employer may with impunity fire his excess. This right is, of course, hotly contested. But in a state college in Illinois recently as many as thirty tenured faculty were axed; Ohio State has announced that thirteen tenured professors will be dropped in academic year 1975-76. Local unions have got into the act.

For, reciprocally, with teacher unions now establishing collective-bargaining contracts with publicly funded higher institutions (as well as high schools), a further cushioning for the guerrilla with tenure is provided. It is a common feature of the latter to criticize teacher unions, which have in fact done much for their membership, until his own job is in jeopardy, and he runs to them squealing for legal help.

With students now made into voting adults, able to vote school boards in or out, the campus is indeed likely to lose its proper configuration and more and more assume that of the society at large. It will cease to be a house of intellect. You will appeal to the police rather than good manners (at Oxford of old it would have been, at worst, the proctors, and no record on the blotter entered). At my own city college it was, after the riots, extremely difficult to ease out several tenure-guerrillas who had incited students to arson. Recourse had to be made to the courts. We heard the equivalent of this indignation— Hey! I'm being fired! Haven't I just served my college signally by trying to burn it down? Both the Bruce Franklin and Jay Schulman cases, at Stanford and CCNY respectively, demonstrated the divisive nature of faculty accord. Schulman, with a beard, a booming voice, and a dog he called Black Boy, was to be found at demonstrations at Columbia when our own campus was in insufficient turmoil; it was some time before we could be rid of this turbulent priest. Franklin, tenured, seemed openly dedicated to the destruction of his university, appearing at his hearing before lifesize photos of Stalin and Mao. A bomb was set to explode outside the home of a professor on the board deliberating his dismissal. Franklin was eventually dismissed, but only after thirty-three long days of hearings and huge legal costs. The Plantagenets might have managed things better.

When it came to the advancement of women, Pottinger began to bog down in deep difficulties and this is doubtless one reason why he left HEW. For women are a majority and sex is not a correlative of race, any more than is weight. Sexual differences, and indifferences, cross-thread races and religions, and some of the bitterest attacks on Fem Lib seem to have come from Black Muslim groups.

Furthermore, in a career of college teaching, I have yet to come across anyone objecting to the hiring of a woman on a liberal arts faculty. Perhaps there are fewer women in Math than in English departments, but this is a heritage of social patterning, rarely the fault, I would think, of a chauvinist chairperson. "We desire to appoint," puts out Claremont Men's College, "a Black or Chicano, preferably female." "Dear Mr. Larschan," begins a letter published in *Commentary;* "It is quite true that we have an opening here and that I have examined your dossier. It is very impressive indeed, and I wish I could invite you to come for an interview. At present, however, our department is interested in the appointment of a woman." "All unfilled positions in the university," runs another such announcement, "must be filled by females or blacks." And still Pottinger was repeatedly assailed by militant women's groups for not having utilized contract suspension in their cause.

Nor is the weight analogy entirely frivolous. The only disqualification I have heard any of my colleagues voice as regards women teachers has been their physical strength. Can they keep class discipline among our kind of unruly, jeering, juiced-up, sexist students? The incidence of rape among our female faculty has increased on campus in recent years, one attractive teacheress being raped in the Ladies' Room of her departmental building. But if you point out that in this case HEW is seemingly trying to put right at one blow a world social injustice, you risk receiving the understandable answer: We have to begin somewhere. To this, however, it is equally logical to retort: Why begin by inflicting injustices on innocent others? Is this public atonement or something? Why deliberately breed *more* oppressed groups? Second, in commencing to right these evident wrongs, why not start on General Motors? Turn Jones and Laughlin into a wailing wall. Why attack the beneficent universities? The answer to the last question is, of course, the point—because they are more vulnerable and *feel more guilty.*

After all, calling a chairman a chairperson isn't such a big deal; and what about that vile sexist *son* in the suffix of the neologism? Should we not talk about chairperdaughter? Altering gender terms (*ter, tey,* and the like have been proposed) may be laudable politics, but has not yet proved an effective desexing device. Turkish is without genders, but the nation is none the less "male chauv" for that. Germany, where a girl is an *it* (*das Fräulein*), is emancipated by comparison. "What in thunder is gained in reversing 'God is He' into 'God is She' except irritating people?" Margaret Mead has asked. "It gets us nowhere. All you get with a reversal is the opposite again." It could be said, however, that it does get you into irritating people; and for some that appears to be the principal object of the exercise.

Today the nature of sexuality is far less secure than it used to be. Congress has voted to make the word *wife* mean *husband* in the case of dependents of veterans. Dr. Ira B. Pauly, Associate Professor of Psychiatry at the University of Oregon Medical School, recently came up with the case of a young woman ("C.K.") who insisted that she was a boy simply because she felt like one. She gave herself a boy's name, flattened her breasts, dressed as a man, and married. What would HEW have done with Dr. Pauly's "C.K."? What, indeed, with those Olympic athletes who thought they were women, were dating steady boyfriends to whom they hoped to be married, but who were classified by medical panels as males (chiefly on the basis of testes concealed in the *labia major*)? These sex tests for women athletes, officially initiated in 1966, prompted one British doctor to declare, "there is no definite line between male and female." There were times, of course, and there are still cultures, where it is a disgrace for the husband if his wife works. Doubtless a disgustingly sexist situation, but why take it out on the universities?

As a matter of fact, it seems that sex quotaism, as presently deployed by the government, derives from a sort of private joke; Howard Smith of the House Rules Committee was so exasperated by Dixiecrat opposition to the Civil Rights Bill in 1964 that he slipped in an amendment to include women under the wing of special federal protection, in line with race, color, and religion, and got a chivalrous bow to his idea. It was not long before minority groups were openly muttering against this powerful feminine competitor for their special privileges. Announcements like the following began to pour out:

> The Faculty of Arts and Sciences of Washington University desires to increase the number of faculty members who are either women or members of minority groups.
> We are looking for *female economists and members of minority groups.*
> The Department of Philosophy at the University of Washington is seeking qualified women and minority candidates for faculty positions at all levels. . . . We desire to appoint a Black or Chicano, preferably female.
> I should very much appreciate it if you could indicate which of your 1972 candidates are either Negro or Mexican-American.

This bleak bulletin board has been analyzed by now, notably by George Roche in *The Balancing Act.* There were no two ways about it. The federal government was not only sponsoring, it was ordering quotas. HEW's uneasy reply was to call these *goals.* But, as Sidney Hook observed, "What is the logical or cognitive difference between saying (1) 'You are to aim at a quota of 20% redheads for your staff within two years,' and (2) 'You are to set as your *goal* recruitment of 20% redheads for your staff within two years'?" To call quotas numerical goals is to call them quotas. The quicksand of terminology is akin to that *agreement* which a university makes to abide by a HEW ruling. How can it do otherwise than agree when HEW can confiscate funds after a thirty-day notice? One is reminded of the so-called *consent decree* an industrial company abides by, after issuing allegedly misleading advertisements. How can this be called *consent* when its only alternative is prosecution by the Federal Trade Commission?

We have seen that at CCNY the administration simply denies that quotas are quotas; harder-headed members of the faculty urged that we call quotas what they were, so that we had an entity we could deal with. One of our student newspapers editorialized: "The President seems bent on defending his program to the last—despite the fact that a high administrative official, Dean Harry Lustig (Liberal Arts and Sciences) claims that the Center has 'always had a 50% quota' for minority students. Dr. Marshak disclaims the existence of any quota, but refuses to release a detailed breakdown of next Fall's entering Biomedical class." *Verb sap.*

These concerns have gone so far by now that even someone's arrest record may not be allowed as a cause to refuse employment for him, unless he is White, because, as Allan Ornstein tells us, "more blacks are arrested than whites, and the result of using such records as criteria would be, in the long run, disadvantageous to Black job applicants. Although the Equal Employment Opportunity Commission concedes that a convicted bank robber may be rejected for a job in a bank, they argue that a convicted rapist or murderer may be hired since the act is not job-related."

By now there can be no doubt but that in academe quotaism of this sort is a new kind of anti-Semitism. Jewish intellectuals know that, by HEW's body-count tactics of university appointment, they are over-represented. Comprising only 3% of the population, that principally in the East, and only three-tenths of 1% of the world's population, they figure strongly on the best college faculties, about half of Columbia's being Jewish, and a high proportion of those, I would conjecture, being WEEJ (White Eastern European Jews).

What is more, such professors remember recent persecutions and limitations that they had to work hard, unaided, to overcome. The first college department I taught in, in America, had but one Jew in it—perhaps a slightly better record than the University of Michigan's exclusion of Roman Catholics for 150 years. Yale Law School abandoned its quota for Jewish applicants only in the 1950's. Now Jews are being told that they are *not* minorities in the intellectual world and that, even if they complain that they are so by population norms, well then, they are over-represented on faculties and need not apply.

So Michael Goldberg, a UCLA Sociology graduate, writes in for a job to Sonoma State College and his principal referee is told: "Mr. Goldberg has not contacted me and I fear that were he to do so we would have no more than pleasant conversation, for we are pledged to the affirmative action policy in our hiring this year." President William J. McGill of Columbia put it unequivocally to a B'nai B'rith dinner in 1973:

> It is only honest to say that Jewish faculty view numerical goals for affirmative action as a thinly veiled revival of anti-Semitism. Jews are represented on university faculties far out of proportion with their representation in the population. Affirmative action goals or

quotas or whatever one calls them . . . can only convince Jewish faculty that an effort is afoot once more to exclude them from universities and that simple excellence no longer counts in matters of university appointments.

It must be said that this new form of anti-Semitism is becoming less and less "thinly veiled" on the urban campus. On our own, predominantly Jewish for over a century, student funds have helped to support (or been confiscated for) student newspapers with, it is supposed, student interests paramount in them, and where would-be journalists can learn their trade. In the spring of 1974 such was the virulence of journalistic anti-Semitism on campus that Jewish students themselves funded a new paper, called *The Source*, to defend the Jewish point of view! A viciously anti-Semitic editorial against this paper then appeared in the student *The Paper*, a Black organ whose contributors had names like Kwame Karikari and Ayad Mohamed and Tawala Kweli, with endless articles on Attica, the "Sharpeville massacre," Angela Davis and Charlene Mitchell.

Funding of *The Paper* appeared mysterious, but almost as soon as it got going our Black Vice-President, Robert Carroll, wrote in a conciliatory letter looking forward to "working with" the editors, while Academic Assistant to the President, Michael F. Shugrue, congratulated all concerned on "the fascinating story and photos on the Tanzania trip" (at a moment when that country was imprecating against international Jewry). Shugrue was then promoted to Dean for Community Relations and Academic Development at CUNY's Richmond College, whose new president had just wrecked the curriculum of my own English Department.

But even the newest of New Leftists on the faculty could not quite stomach sponsored anti-Semitism and said so in the student press. Called to account, and asked to apologize, the editors of *The Paper* were unregenerate; they refused to climb down. They said they "endorsed" *The Source* but it was clear they scarcely knew what that term meant. Here is a sample of *The Paper*'s prose relevant to its anti-Semitic article (4/25/74):

> If white people to exist to define all, there must be some who exist not to define anything: people of color.
>
> A recent example of this white perception is the actions taken by *The Source,* a Jewish newspaper, relative to the editorial of *The Paper.*
>
> *The Paper* endorsed *The Source,* meaning *The Paper* had the power to endorse. *The Source* welcomed the "support" of *The Paper,* meaning *The Paper* did not have the power to endorse. Thus the whites of *The Source* redefined the actions of people of color of *The Paper,* in order to perpetuate the myth of the powerlessness of people of color. Another example of this insistence on definition is the recent statement by Robert Marshak that Bernard Sohmer was being replaced as Vice-Provost of Student Affairs, because people of color insisted on having a person of color at this position. But everyone understands that this public position is inconsistent with the mind of Robert Marshak since people of color have no power to define anything; for definition is a pervue [*sic*] of white people only. Thus the white mind of Robert Marshak defined the replacement Bernard Sohmer as an act in the common good of white people.

This is not a roulette board on which you can win. Sohmer was a White Jewish Dean fired, or eased out, by Marshak in favor of a minority replacement. The classification implicit in quotaism of this sort compels us to ignore the dissimilarities in equivalents. Whenever a class ends up meaning more than it generalizes (Communism, pornography), it is but a whirling word. At the time Marshak was being assailed for racism by *The Paper,* while trying in fact to be more liberal and less racist than anyone around, the poor man was confronted with an obscene cartoon of a nun masturbating with a crucifix in another student newspaper, called *Observation Post.*

This patent steal from *The Exorcist* was mischievously calculated to offend both Catholics and women (not to mention those who knew anything about drawing). Catholics have to date been remarkably restrained in secular higher education, where they have received repeated abuse; on this occasion I am happy to say I helped crank up the Catholic hierarchy to respond to this gratuitous insult, yet despite the efforts of Father O'Gara, in charge of our college's Catholic Center, the President did nothing about the offense and no apology was forthcoming. Most students were either sickened or bored by the moronic ineptitude of the whole thing, not to say lack of manners. Catholics comprise 30% of the population and, if you include Hispanics, a probably larger percentage of the minority population. Why has not HEW required to see them proportionately represented on college faculties?

Massive federal aid for higher education was obviously not going to go out without some strings attached; in fact, now that those strings have begun to manipulate the puppets of our college administrations, more than one critic has echoed Paul Seabury's realization that there must be "some among the President's Republican equerry who take perverse pleasure in watching academic liberals, crusaders for social justice for others, now hoist by their own petard on home territory." For if you are truly intent on controlling higher education, the next stage is to check party cards, as in Russia or China.

Teaching in a department of around two hundred, I much doubt if a single one of my colleagues voted Republican with the majority of America. At one point my Chairman took the trouble to circulate the information that I had—*horresco referens*—actually written for *National Review*. What crime could be worse? But it is one on the decrease these days since rapidly extirpated. Ronald Berman describes one method by which this is managed at the University of California at San Diego:

> a faculty member who ventured to teach, although he did not support, the Jensen hypothesis was harassed by a coalition of student groups. Upon appeal to the administration, he was informed that he had only these alternatives: to clear the lectures with his antagonists; to debate them instead of carrying on his lectures; to give up his lectures; to endure harassment.

Or maybe leave for Cuba. Better still, Japan, where the university is, in Jacques Barzun's words, "a little totalitarian state under the dictatorship of the students, abetted by those faculty members whose politics jibe with theirs." Among the alternatives mentioned to Berman, the administration did not allow *to give harassment back.*

It is difficult to poll the political attitudes of professors, and the matter of their leanings in this area has remained a notoriously thorny one. However, the Carnegie Commission's recent survey of 60,000 faculty members was probably the most comprehensive in this regard to date; it found 70% of those in History, English, Sociology, Psychology, Philosophy, Political Science, and Economics openly labeling themselves as liberal or radical; only Agriculture, Engineering, and Physical Education came out as predominantly conservative.

With our economics professors "radical" we surely see our social suicide in a nutshell, since our government funds men and women to detest the private enterprise system. John Searle of the University of California in Berkeley writes, "I can testify from personal experience that many of the same faculty members who vigorously defended the rights of Professor Angela Davis, when the Regents attempted to fire her for her political views, showed no interest in the case (one of many, I might add) of Professor Robert Scalapino, whose class was disrupted by left-wing students."

Edward Rozek, a University of Colorado, Boulder, professor, would go even further, calling our colleges today "staging areas for an assault upon free society." In a Report of the Cornell Alumni Committe for Balanced Education we read:

> For the past three or four decades the majority of the professors in the social sciences have been of the liberal and collectivist persuasions. Thus we have had an entire generation of college graduates enter their careers, including teaching, with the views of our society and economy which their liberal professors have imparted to them.

Lawrence Fertig, a member of the Board of Trustees of New York University for eighteen years, endorses this opinion: "in many departments of American universities, such as economics, sociology, history and the other so-called social sciences, the ideological content taught to students is entirely one-sided. It is of the modern liberal persuasion."

Interestingly, a 1970 *Educational Reviewer* survey of student opinion, polling twelve universities on views about religious affiliations for Presidency, found the only strong objection to a Jew receiving that appointment coming from Howard University, a predominantly Black college in Washington, D.C. In fact, an upperclass sample found an *increase* of 3% in this objection by Howard as compared with a similar survey made there seven years earlier. Sixteen percent of those newly polled at Howard now object to the idea of a Jew as President; none of the other colleges sampled (from Stanford to Yale) came anywhere near this, not a single one of them even near double figures. Howard's reaction here was extraordinary.

To conclude, the massive Kennedy-Johnson educational program started on its way a steamroller that was paternalistic in inception, a very condescending machine indeed. It may have abounded in good intentions, but in the colleges it paved our hell with those. The U.S. Peace Corps was regularly spat upon, in one corner of the globe or another. Daniel Moynihan writes: "Remember the great thrust for Headstart? There is recently very clear evidence that this kind of education and experience has no educational consequences of any kind except for the Hunter College graduates who become Headstart teachers." The same with our SEEK.

Bureaucracy of the monolithic HEW-OCR type, with employees running into the thousands, has an inevitably self-serving, leveling effect. You end up realizing that HEW is really attacking the principle of higher education, and condescending to the new open admissions students coming into it; as Paul Seabury has put it, "one bad turn deserves another." Now that your students are less qualified, they only deserve less qualified faculty. T. S. Eliot was not far wrong when he wrote that "in our headlong rush to educate everybody, we are lowering the standards. . . .destroying our ancient edifices to make ready the ground upon which the barbarian nomads of the future will encamp in their mechanized caravans."

Epilogue: Down with Us!

Rush Welter once wrote that to understand America one must understand the way her people have thought about education. At the moment they appear to regard it as a sort of magic, and to extend it as the way to solve every social problem. America possesses the most elaborate educational system in the world, with the average of school years completed rising higher than that of any other major economy in the world. Not only Japan, but several leading European nations thrive on far lower educational profiles.

The present study, gloomy as it may have been at times, has been an attempt to further this understanding of the nation's culture through its thinking about education. In the course of it we have inspected what seem to be deliberate symptoms of the academic death wish. Preaching to under-privileged youth that America is "total lethal evil," and annually reshaping your curriculum to that end, merely serve to disrupt yet further what are already fragile social ties. Here, in what might be called the end of education in all senses, that moment of pause in which true learning should take place, we find institution after institution overthrowing itself from within. What looks, at first glance, like a progressive widening of opportunity soon turns into its opposite as values are eroded and derided, and the entire social structure is gleefully, stage

231

by stage, dismantled. Butler's Colleges of Unreason are here, and they look as if they might be here to stay.

We have seen the imposition of requirements in college, finally of any curriculum at all in the true sense of that term, regarded as authoritarian, arbitrary, and to be abandoned, except in the sciences. We have seen an increase in sheer numbers making for a decline in standards and leading to rioting and crime. As cure, an adoration of criminality under various guises (subventioned subversion) and still more and more egalitarianism, leading to the undermining of the Constitution itself by government as its agencies seek to impose quotas.

With the desire for survival locally so low, nothing seems to stop this self-righteous march of so-called liberalism toward its own destruction. Forever abolishing the Bourbons, our perfervid intellectuals are all busily weaving the noose for their own necks. Malcolm Muggeridge summarized the situation in *Esquire*:

> we have been forced to finance, and sometimes defend, dema-gogue-dictators of the most unedifying kind, who have ridden to power on the one-man-one-vote principle so dear to our liberal hearts. It is a case of responsibility without power—the opposite of the prerogative of the harlot. A similar process may be detected at work in America, whereby the liberal mind's proneness to excessive guilt feelings has induced so fawning and sycophantic an attitude toward Negro discontent and subversion that lifelong white agitators for civil rights, inveterate freedom-marchers and admirers of Martin Luther King, integrationists who have squatted and howled and been carried screaming away by the police for years past, nowadays find themselves being kicked in the teeth by Black Panthers and other Negro militants with a ferocity which might seem excessive directed against the reddest of red-necks.

Capitulation never helped a Jacobin keep his neck clear of the guillotine, nor a Bolshevik out of the Lubyanka. As our own college administration was allocating money for Black student visits to Zambia and Tanzania and other spots (where they proved, by the by, far from welcome), the Sixth Pan-African Congress, ending in Tanzania on June 27th, 1974, issued a General Declaration whose main point was the *rejection* of Black Power (to date, I have seen no special funding for our students to visit Israel).

One could further add that New York as a city has certainly fallen over backwards to try to assist its Spanish-speaking citizens. Signs are not co-written in Algerian in Paris nor in Gaelic in the Hebrides, nor does Singapore require all its teachers to learn Chinese. In 1896 an Aide to the Mayor of New York wrote, "In some districts there are vast throngs of foreigners where one scarcely hears a word of English spoken; where the mode of living is repugnant to every American idea. The best interests of the city demand that children of such a population be brought under American influences and instruction." Dark days, indeed.

The educational egalitarian, in the words of Angus Maude, "instinctively dislikes any process which enables some children to emerge markedly ahead of their fellows." He is not an educator, he is a trainer; in fact John Dewey used these terms coterminously, interchangeably (as in his attack on Albert Jay Nock). The American university was seen by such men as Dewey as a generalizing force, working horizontally rather than vertically. If it seems hard to take exception to this, try continuing it to the conclusion of a Buell Gallagher, who defines the "obligation of the institution" as "to facilitate the expression of the Beloved Community" (his capitals). It has been quite extraordinary how many ecclesiastical or clerical voices have lately contributed, on both sides of the Atlantic, to this most brutal materialism of our times. In Yeats's words, they "thirst for accusation."

It is true that this materialism was early normative in American higher education which, even by 1918, Thorstein

Veblen had criticized for its "businessman mentality." One assumes that this trend was excusable. James Truslow Adams tells us that in the early American colonies "the educational system, devised for the people by the people, did not aim at training either mind or character, but only at instilling facts useful for making a living." This is a long way from J. C. Masterman, indeed. It forgets that in a true democracy everyone is called on to vote, to participate indirectly in matters of public policy; training people in occupational skills is simply not enough. The resultant irony latent in the present book was a fact of New York City schools, so admirably charted by Diane Ravitch in *The Great School Wars*, from the start; originally they were organized along ward lines, only to be "freed" from politics by reformers like Columbia's Nicholas Murray Butler who pinned their faith on the centralizing professional administrator; in a Hegelian twist, this element in the educational process has now grown hydra-headed and ultrapolitical.

As tentatively suggested in the first chapter, the problem of higher education in America is that, *ipso facto*, the university is not a democratic body. Oxbridge never pretended to be anything other than an institution devoted to intellectual values. It served as brain-box for a more or less viable civilization (and it is incorrect to allege that it was the preserve of the rich, except during a period of decadence in the eighteenth century). America has insisted on all its institutions being "democratic," in a rigorous sense, with the inherent fallacy, spouted at us by clergymen like Buell Gallagher and the Bishop of Woolwich, that the university should be a replica of the national participatory democracy. Everyone should then immediately vote on what type of elevators to install, and how best to flush the maintenance men's john. Everyone should go on strike, too, whenever a cafeteria worker is fired. You are part of the social structure. Shape up, or else.

But even John Dewey, dear heart, did not envisage the university as quite this tough, power-grabbing replica of the national political body, writing at one point: "Belief in equality is an element of the democratic credo. It is not, however, belief in equality of natural endowments. Those who proclaimed the idea of equality did not suppose they were enunciating a psychological doctrine, but a legal and political one."

If, as has been said, the university enters politics, then politics will enter the university. We have witnessed this in no uncertain terms in the action of HEW: today's Banford or Jensen could well be tomorrow's Charles Reich or Germaine Greer. If you charge into society head-on in the manner exemplified above of students, then society is going to ask some accounting of your actions. "It seems quite absurd to expect," writes Henry Novotny, "that the society would tolerate and finance, under the guise of academic freedom, supposedly educational institutions that would, in fact, be training grounds for hostile guerrillas and totalitarian fanatics." If the university is a participatory democracy, why should not presidents be elected by the students, on a four-year basis? Clark Kerr, Grayson Kirk, and Nathan Pusey—to cite three celebrated instances—weren't much more enduring. Why should not the nearest janitor have a one-vote say in the election?

So it becomes a matter of national character, of style, to which element you give priority. Shortly after the Second World War the U. S. Labor Department announced that, on average, college graduates would earn $100,000 more in their lifetimes than if they had gone out into the world with only high school diplomas. Today such income differentials have largely disappeared. When I first taught engineering students at CCNY I knew that, on graduation, most of them would at once get jobs worth double my salary. Today, with college education whittled down to the shadow of the prestige it once enjoyed, noncollege graduates have far more of a chance in the labor force than before.

A generalized concept of national character for Americans has been a notorious pitfall in sociology. Nevertheless, Helen Merrell Lynd ventures, in her book on the search for identity, that what distinguishes us from other peoples is "a tendency to believe that to every problem there is a here-and-now right or best answer, and that if one acts in terms of the right answer one's efforts should meet with success."

To one who has spent a life's work in higher education in America, those words are for the tombstone; certainly they apply fully to the collapse of the curriculum inspected above. There "right answers" come up annually, daily. If Black Studies are deserted, and a rally of students has to take place, as one such did in front of our Morris Cohen Library, protesting "lack of student input" in the program, then you must come up with another "right answer." Pragmatically, you must alter your courses. "If China becomes Communist," Mrs. Lynd goes on, "we do not study the history of China; we ask through whose villainy we 'lost' China."

But now that America is so materially rich and powerful, and can physically blow itself off the face of the earth if it wishes, it would seem a pity to continue what has become so much spiritual suicide. For educationally we are today at a crossroads, trying to worship both God and Mammon. As Peter Witonski puts it, "Universities cannot serve two masters: they cannot exist as employment agencies and educational institutions at the same time." On the one hand, we have seen an institution like CUNY claiming to be helping the underprivileged into society, even into positions of power in that society; on the other, we have watched it so diluting its degree that the place has turned into little more than a diploma mill.

New York is now spending more money than any other state on education (nearly $2,000 a year on every student attending a public school in 1971). But the mere pouring of money into education does not ensure that our children will be educated. It does not even necessarily ensure that they will be successful citizens, later on, in the host culture. After all, one assumes that someone is going to have to live in New York State, and California, rather than Togo Togoland. To urge these "ghetto kids" into African and Boricuan Studies (as Puerto Rican Studies are now called by *independistas*) may be as much of a hindrance as a help.

In which connection it can be seen how harmoniously the Puerto Rican minority of New York City, generally active and hard-working, has blended in with the host culture without sacrificing its own. Apart from a few student agitators, they have not made the fantastic demands for "reparations" of the Black minority. During the college riots of the sixties, indeed, it was a source of constant fury to campus Blacks that they could not organize Puerto Ricans under their banner. There were occasions when they did so, but many more when they failed, and our own Black student paper, eager to exploit any mischief in this area, now seems to have given up the struggle.

That the American society is so intent on sponsoring its own destruction may be due to a variety of reasons. Our democracy has grown so plural and "open" of late that its self-destructions will usually be more arresting than its contributions. You make more noise hating someone or something than expressing affection or satisfaction. Our opinions, writes Daniel Boorstin, "are distinguished by the strength with which they are held rather than by the

authenticity with which their conclusions are demonstrable.''
It was to be observed that our late flower children, chanting
peace and fingering love beads, were adept at blowing up
buildings, if sometimes themselves in them. "Democratic
societies," Boorstin goes on, "tend to become more concerned
with what people believe than what is true." This seems just;
we even judge art by what it does rather than by what it is.
Here the university should stand as a bulwark for "what is
true." Instead, we overcommunicate, and thus dilute and
attenuate all the time. The Pentagon sold its version of the
Vietnam war like a deodorant and was proud of it.' The
demeaning of meaning may proceed apace in our midst, but it
is singularly suicidal to urge on this process from, of all
places, the academy.

Surely the evidence above has shown us by now that
capitulation to unreason only produces more of the same, as
in the backfiring of HEW's beneficence. This folly was seldom
more succinctly seen than in the short history, to date, of the
Free University of Berlin, today the very antithesis of "free."
Founded by the U. S. Government in conjunction with the
Ford Foundation after the Second World War, this has now
become the most violent and American-hating campus in
Europe, its students, drawn mainly from the middle classes,
shooting American soldiers in the back and beating up their
professors in the street when not hurling sacks of flour at such
unlikely characters as the Shah of Iran.

According to Henry F. May, Margaret Byrne Professor of
History at the University of California, Berkeley, the most
strongly felt role for the American university today is "the
civic or moral." There are those of us who have had to live this
role to its *reductio* in America's largest city, where education
has come to be regarded as part of the free social services, like
vaccination, and your treatment of the "facilities" at a city

college therefore akin to those at Orchard Beach. " 'A year of graduate work' has become in the United States a social form," writes Jacques Barzun, "like a shower for the bride." The valuation placed on the degree is then seen as your fault.

Arnold Beichman says that our college faculties have by now decided "that for the foreseeable future the university is no longer a place where truth is to be pursued. What has been tacitly ratified is a decision that the American university is primarily (not secondarily) the springboard for upward social mobility as the ascriptive right for ethnic minorities." Addressing himself to the logical question as to why all Americans should not be given a Ph.D. at birth, Professor S. M. Miller recently told the American Orthopsychiatric Association that "we have become a credential society in which one's educational level is more important than what he can do."

But this turning to "the civic or moral" has had its distinct penalties. Barzun claims that "as welfare functions increase the removal of ignorance declines." At the end of a lifetime of municipal education in America I sometimes wonder if the administration of state and urban universities would not be better under direct popular control, and legislation. Rather than under such intermediary bodies as New York City's Board of Higher Education or the notorious California Regents, I feel I could have done my job with more confidence and security under the personal aegis of the taxpayer: of Angelo, the Puerto Rican proprietor of the "Thrifty" Supermarket where my wife and I do most of our shopping; of Bill, the Black maintenance man of our building with a daughter going through Hofstra; of Herbie, our Jewish butcher who somehow or other survived both Arno and Rapido crossings in World War Two; and Louie, our Italo-American fruit-and-vegetable man. I much doubt if any of the above would have allowed the excesses of our student riots and they would certainly not have sat down to "negotiate" with the rioters. I realize that this may be but to rephrase William Buckley's comment that he would rather be governed by the first hundred people in the Boston Telephone Directory than by the faculty of Harvard College, yet how many at Harvard today might agree with him?

As one reaches the end of a dossier of intellectual decadence as depressing as that of this book has been, one wants to know *Why*? At least, one does if one feels any fraternity at all with this large population of academic authorities; the other course is simply to see the whole escapade as hilariously funny. After all, these determined professors, so vociferously wishing well, are human beings, and some of them are said to be the sages of the Western world. God help the West if so, but it is incumbent on a critic to drive more deeply into the springs that supply this so incontestable flock of tax-supported progressives, our hydra-headed college faculties, each spawning yet another intellectual masochist ready to lie on his back and beg his oppressor, *Kick me harder—please*. In short, to ask why the manifest death wish has been so successful in our academies over the past decade.

For it cannot be said that this group is a cadre with a very high reputation for political prognosis, exactly. It was wrong about Stalin, it was wrong about Ulbricht, Castro, Allende, and the rest, and now the old lags who spent the last half of their lives cursing Stalin for taking them in are seeing a similar infatuation with China on the part of young American intellectuals. After all, the SDS originally supported Lyndon Johnson, no less. Psychology Professor Henry R. Novotny, of California State at Bakersfield, is explicit on the subject: "I believe the blame for most of this century's massacres should be placed primarily on aberrant intellectuals, not on so-called military establishments."

I do not know whether this emotionalism is particularly American or not; certainly it was said that the Russophobia of the McCarthy fifties was impelled by the Russophilia of the last years of the Second World War, a sort of political equivalent of the reaction of a teenager turned down by his latest girl friend. The analogy is not beside the point. English politics of the time had normally conceived of Russians as rogues (Joseph Conrad's view of them) and the volte-face after the war was less wounding to national self-esteem. Having been brought up to consider Stalin a base tyrant, I was baffled, when arriving in America in those years, to be beaten over the head by *Partisan Review* liberals into a view my generation in England had always held. Today one sometimes wonders whether, for the current crop of liberals, almost anywhere that is not America is better than America.

However, it cannot be said that England, either, escaped the implications of its own liberal death wish. Generally speaking, the British technique was to anesthetize dissent by promoting it into incorporation in the English way of life—play cricket with them, be beaten by them on the race-track (as by the Aga Khan), strew knighthoods and OBE's about on almost everyone, notably on members of nations that had hated you. It is probably now forgotten, even in England, how bitterly someone like the graceful Nehru held the English up to loathing.

Perhaps this technique worked up to a point, but England cannot be exculpated; it also, in the thirties, had an intelligentsia that adulated what was, in fact, a brutal authoritarianism. Stephen Spender, John Lehmann, and the rest of the parlor pinks of the period made grotesque political miscalculations, for which a younger generation had to pay. In

New Writing in Europe (1940) Lehmann made this confession relevant to the efficacy of his generation as political barometer:

> I think it is hardly an exaggeration to say that the arrival of the great Soviet films of the "epic" period in London, films such as *Mother, The General Line, Storm Over Asia, Earth,* was an event which had a decisive formative influence on the minds of the most alert of the new generation.

How alert were they? For Stephen Spender's essay in *The God That Failed* reiterates this romantic excitement, his movie list being *"Earth, Potemkin, Mother, Turksib, Ten Days That Shook the World, The Way Into Life."* The formation of your politics by seeing films is not a very encouraging intellectual quotient, but our student programs today, with *The Battle of Algiers* on at Repeat, are doing the same. So the question has to be answered. Malcolm Muggeridge tells us:

> Never, our archaeologists of the future will surely conclude, was any generation of men intent upon the pursuit of happiness more advantageously placed to attain it, who yet, with seeming deliberation, took the opposite course—toward chaos, not order; toward breakdown, not stability; toward death, destruction and darkness, not life, creativity and light.

Why?

To begin with, the liberal clearly feels purged of social sin by all the strenuous do-goodism instanced above; the nearest Ethnic Studies Department is his equivalent of Right Guard. This is not an intellectual motive. The drive to damage oneself is a complex procedure but in the present context a second answer as to why it takes place today in academe might be developed from Kenneth Keniston's theory of "red-diaper" babies. Keniston feels that the war in Vietnam had little to do with the true thrust behind campus unrest in the sixties; any other event could have triggered it off at the time. His "red-diaper" babies were our deans, the Spocked generations, in particular those whose parents and grandparents had been through the Depression and who came out of World War Two with social goals that could be achieved only via violence and revolution. They were, in short, our anti-intellectuals.

In fact, the American academic situation is, viewed from certain angles, less irrational than it looks. The "high incidence of anti-intellectuals in intellectual roles" in American society is explained by Morse Peckham in terms of the children's game of Prisoner's Base. His lengthy and delightfully convoluted analogy boils down to the suggestive suggestion that in this game (or social structure) children simultaneously enact the roles of transgressor *and* policeman. They respect the rules of the game even as they infringe them and are hostile to any attempts to modify them.

So with our city college professor. He remains quite indifferent when you show him that his pseudo-revolutionary or "transgressive" educational premises are preposterous and impossible; and he is a very exacting policeman when you get caught in his territory. On the one hand, he promotes social instability (in the choice of courses, texts, heroes, campus speakers, socially validated incompetence); on the other, since there is virtually no such thing as society in a city like New York today, and the police are practically apologetic, the pseudo-revolutionary is suddenly in a position of power and can, in education at any rate, exercise arbitrary actions (ethnic studies, quotas) in the spirit of an academic *Gauleiter.*

You can, and probably must, then point out to these anti-intellectuals every reason why they should abandon their destructive educational dogmas. But to do so makes no dent on the advancing juggernaut. They are defending not reason but a belief system and, as Professor Peckham puts it, "To the anti-intellectual, beliefs do not have to be rational to be valuable, they merely have to be beliefs." Hence, like the addict's, this kind of professor's dependence on that which punishes and destroys him, the spuriously "revolutionary" student body. One anti-intellectual dogma lives comfortably with another and it is pointless to point out all the absurdities and inconsistencies. By now we have seen how SDS has become a mirror image of John Birchism with, perhaps, an even sharper flair for violence than that creed's. When the notes I had painstakingly accumulated over decades were destroyed by students, who then set up their own university, I learned—the hard way—that these transgressors were not in the least interested in tolerant inquiry but rather in taking over police power in the field themselves. That they have now largely done so has been the principal burden of this book.

In the days of the worst City College riots, I recall reporting for nonexistent classes, pushing past the hate-filled faces screaming and yelling under sundry placards at the college gates—MONSTERS OF ALL KINDS MUST BE DESTROYED, Mao Tse-tung, or Orwellian efforts like DOWN WITH JUSTICE!—and wondering what the new Nonnegotiable Demand today was to be, and whether that was Lionel Trilling hanging in effigy by the Student Center, and then clearing my head and recollecting that there was a fashionable professor in our department who wrote for *Vogue* on the side, who had lately written a book about Mao and his numbingly banal "thoughts," and sold it to the movies, too, under the Bloody Yoke of Capitalist Colonialism.

Then I looked back at the platoons of gum-chewing cops standing there in the rain, Fascist Nazi Imperialist Hyena Pigs and Decadent Running Dogs of U. S. Colonialism from Brooklyn and the Bronx and Harlem and the Lower East Side, standing there pot-bellied and patient and bored, waiting out the screaming hate and obscene signboards and contorted

faces of yet another "peaceful demonstration" permitted by
the city, hoping that today at least they might not be
expectorated upon or urinated upon or kicked in the groin by
one of their own kids encouraged to the task by a bearded
professor drawing double their city salary, or, better, be
spared having sulphuric acid thrown in their faces, while the
peace-loving liberal reporters and television men looked on in
the interests of free, impartial news.

And I must say I couldn't help thinking at such moments
of how they did it in Mao's China itself. As I passed my first
wandering junkie, helplessly giggling with himself, I realized
that in New York City we are supposed to feel *sorry* for
addicts. In Mao's China they don't have a drug problem
because they shot all the addicts, presumably on the premise
that you can't be an addict if you're dead. They also shoot the
hundreds of thousands who annually dare to try to escape
their beloved chairman's Earthly Paradise and make it across
the border into decadent colonial dung-hills like Hong-Kong.
When these misguided people are returned, they are publicly
executed, with or without a spell in a Thought Reform Labor
Camp, white dunce-caps on their heads, to the clapping of
collected villagers plus many readings from the smiling Mao
After which, it's back to work in those commune paddy fields,
and better keep in with your children, Comrade, since these
days they get paid for denouncing their parents, with a bonus
for flogging their teachers through the streets or burning
priceless art works in museums. We were not entirely exempt.
We had our equivalent of Mao-think sessions, too. TRUST
THE MASSES!

It has all been a painful case of Durkheimian anomie.
In a rapidly expanding economy huge hopes were held out and
when these could not be approached, let alone attained, you
relapsed into a Flaubertian cynicism (the Silent Generation) or
simply tried to get them by force. In Mao's China, after this or

that Great Leap Forward (MORE BETTER CHEAPER FASTER!) you could simply execute a lot of people. Fortunately, you couldn't in America. Nonetheless, our civic universities have developed their own Little Red Books.

One rule in ours ran:

"What does a venerable senior Full Professor call a surly Black Freshperson who insists on addressing him, 'You motherfucker'?"

"He calls him Sir."

The gap between the American dream and reality, constantly enlarged by the media exaggerations and aggravated by advertising, was simply too great. I confess to being persuaded of this as a conceivable motive for the otherwise totally suicidal behavior of some of my colleagues; often decent people, they have, however, come out of very moderate, even lower-class homes, and to be able to lean down and give a hand up to someone evidently *beneath* them (the "ghetto kids") confers intoxicating social graces.

Then there is the messianic fervor, already touched on in these pages; it is quite real and an important element for anyone embarking on an academic career today to understand. Education is not primarily reform, but urban America has made it so. Teach in a large municipal college for a while and you will realize that your colleagues are not principally embarked on intellectual inquiry, but on a *cause*. It is that of the nineteenth-century British missionary, bringing "light" into "darkness" and attacking the good God Shiva at Hindu festivals and getting a thrill whenever one misguided devotee out of millions throws a stone. Shivaism is advanced by the attack and Grove Press waits in the wings with a book on the cult. Horace Mann was of this stamp; in letters to men like Dr. Barnard of Columbia (who asked "Why waste a thousand-dollar education on a five-dollar boy?") Mann talked about education as his "religion," and likened himself to an ancient Crusader.

Finally, if you wish to understand the true dynamic of the academic death wish, you must acknowledge that, in Helen Merrell Lynd's words, "Guilt, at least in our culture, can be a form of communication." So can shame, and self-punishment. With open admissions, and the arrival in urban academe of large, indeed overwhelming, numbers of hostile mental children who can barely communicate among themselves, the intellectual *communicates by guilt*. Horrified to find himself so cut off from people who are, he must admit, fellow human beings, be beats his breast, cries out to the skies that it was all his fault, and asks to have "reparations" imposed on himself. It is a depressing spectacle. And if one were asked, justifiably enough, for remedies to redress some of the evils and arrogances depicted in this book, first and foremost among them would be to reverse this self-destructive strain in the academic psyche.

It would *not* be simply to go on pouring more and more money into the cracks in the dike. As we have seen in the tragic elimination of minority cultures in Scotland and Ireland—more particularly the former since it never achieved any genuine political independence—nationalizing or federalizing education saps local cultures, eradicates individual differences, and deprives large numbers of people of dignity and drive. The Gaelic-speaking Scot, like the Corse-speaking Corsican, was made into a figure of fun on the vaudeville stage of the common culture; such oddities got in the way, of BBC and RTF alike.

In America we have seen how more federal money means, educationally, less local control. The result is such homogeneity that Peter Witonski writes, "the Office of Education has developed into a kind of sociological police force, determined to equalize *all* American education, whatever the cost in money and suffering." To this one can only add that, tragically enough, such steamrollering is precisely what the city liberal is after, also. He does not want *individual* Puerto Ricans, he does not want Alabaman and Georgian and Jamaican Blacks, he wants groups he can move around and herd behind his back, in the manner of HEW. He wants socialism—by which I mean a cultural pattern assumed as normal and desirable because a majority practices it (as in National Socialism).

Nor would an educational panacea be to appoint yet more Deans, even more highly paid, new Vice-Vice-Provosts and Sub-Deputy Chairpersons, to administer still more "programs." College administration has recently ranked as the most rapidly expanding profession in the nation's history. It is going to help no one to send up yet more agencies and departments, forever answering the nearest needs. No more blueprints, no more supersuperuniversities.

One thing to do would be to drop the term *dropout*. This is a shame coining from the liberal lexicon, and it has been successful enough to spark off national campaigns. To decline to continue sitting in an overcrowded classroom for no particularly useful purpose for an extra four years, principally to support a philosophy of education, should not be classified as shirking. Dropouts of past decades are apparently doing much better in American society than the highly educated of the same era. Simply to extend years of schooling, now into the so-called colleges, will not ensure a higher cultural level in the country as a whole.

But more and more schooling is at present the universal panacea, notably against racial discrimination. It is, writes George Pettitt, "a house of magic where, presumably, genetic endowment, personality aberrancies, and motivational limitations can all be reconstituted so as to conform more closely to the nation's ego-ideal." Increasing the retention power of the schools, turning public colleges into what Charles Frankel calls "holding institutions for people past seventeen," may in fact be rather less idealistic than its proponents make it sound, being, in short a *sub rosa* method of policing the labor market. For the liberal is also in the business of keeping unemployment from becoming unmanageable; this would seem somewhat cynical, but a recent Secretary of Labor openly declared that "education is the answer to unemployment" in this spirit.

Shaming youngsters to stay in school simply because their needs will remain unmet in the society at large is singularly myopic, and must lead to large-scale anomie, 25% of all arrests in the United States involving juveniles under twenty-one, and our suicide rate soaring over twenty thousand a year (exclusive of abortive attempts and so-called accidents). Extending education has now become part of America's mythology, and nobody seems able to stop it. It is a probably tragic cultural delusion.

As a matter of fact, the liberal's true elitism can be seen in this induction of shame in the young, in whom is being inculcated a contempt for those with limited ability or in "inferior" jobs. It could be said that what our city colleges are engaged in is making their students permanently ashamed of their parents—for holding the jobs they do. The first thing a city college does is to fracture the student's family. These students are then told that the only way to succeed is through more and more education whereupon, lo and behold, all will suddenly be equal. The top of the pyramid up which they are cajoled into climbing is suddenly, instead of a peak, a long and level plateau where all are essentially back at base, since there are no jobs around, or increasingly fewer of them, for the long-distance toilers of this educational elite. Here wanders a very lonely crowd, indeed. George Pettitt well puts it that "anyone who promises a potential dropout from high school a greater chance of finding work if he suffers through two or three more years of high school is ignoring the facts."

By lowering the educational requirements and standards of our colleges, as I have instanced above, the liberal educator imagines that he is helping youth along this assembly line into society, lending a hand, when in fact he is damaging that youth by pemitting such lax work habits that job-holding, if and when it occurs, will prove very onerous. Lack of rigor in the curriculum is what really generates boredom, and if students are deserting college, it is because they are not being intellectually challenged or spiritually stimulated.

Let us, then, at least begin the repair job with Daniel Boorstin's principle, "abandon the prevalent belief in the superior wisdom of the ignorant." Then staff your liberal arts, at least, with those who believe in them. It is fairly clear that the government does not believe in this area of study. When the National Endowment of the Humanities was created, largely at the instigation of President Johnson, in 1965, it was hoped that this agency would help, rather than hinder, the humanities. Mel A. Topf, however, in a trenchant article in *College English* for November 1975, summarizes the grants given to date by NEH and finds few of them having much to do with the humanities at all.

The sizable grants have gone to social-science projects, for example, "Race and Class in an Urban Complex" (Northwestern), "Workshop in Black Expression and Experience" (Pitzer College, California). Even family planning grants have been made under this heading—"The Relationship between Contraception and Personal Integrity" —while over $600,000 was given to Tufts for a program in "Civil and Foreign Affairs." Other funded projects in the period have included conferences on gerontology and a play "on the continuing patterns of racism in Rhode Island." For so-called interdisciplinary freshman seminars in "urban poverty" and "the military-industrial complex," $227,000 was given to Wilmington College.

Complete confusion about what the humanities are or may be seems to exist within NEH, which sees them generally in a civic role, as when a "humanities curriculum for young criminal offenders" was funded at Penn State. Needless to say, this mimicry of the social sciences only further dilutes and destroys the humanities, Professor Topf wisely concluding: *"Does* government have a role to play in helping the humanities through dark times? I think not. The fragments which remain of the destroyed humanist tradition are too fragile to withstand the pressures which come from government influence."

And these pressures are increasing. Acceptance of almost any government aid now generally involves administrations in the Kafkaesque world of regulatory agencies and their infinite rules, attendant on such benefice. A recent American Council on Education study shows crippling costs to colleges involved in Federal programs. Here financial assistance slinks in, loosely cloaking social goals, the price for which turns out to be heavy, ranging from Social Security taxes to costly compliance with a very wide range of requirements. Two colleges—Brigham Young in Utah and Hillside in Michigan— recently refused such compliance, as exceeding the government's authority. In 1974 Dartmouth declined 6,300 applicants and then had to face an extremely costly Federal fiat of keeping a file for three years on every candidate rejected for admission.

Would the path elected by Brigham Young and Hillside be to do even as Oxford did? What matter, if so? We should be willing to learn from truly learned institutions. J. C. Masterman was an exceptionally rational human being. Finally, I might even recommend getting back into the urban academic fold some genuine eccentrics, perhaps even a few of those outrageous enough to feel that America represents one of the most optimistic experiments in human history, plus a real attempt at a multiracial community. Obviously, any enemy can write this off as superpatriotism. It seems a risk worth taking with the gospel going the other way, and anything faintly supportive of America being ridiculed and discredited in liberal academe. But the chief remedial action must be *to get politics out of the university*. In our cities there are few indications, however, of this direction.

DATE DUE